All Things
Wise and Wonderful

by

Mildred Pratt

Barratt Ministries Publications
Manchester M14 5QH, England

Contents

Prologue

This book is an autobiographical sketch of the life of Miss Mildred Pratt, MBE, often affectionately known as 'Millie'.

Her story takes us from a home in Nelson, Lancashire, England, to the remote bush area of northwest Zambia; from the rain and cotton mills to the sun and heat of the Copper Belt; from being a school teacher to becoming an ambassador and witness to the saving grace and power of her Lord Jesus Christ to thousands. Displaying a passion, determination, commitment and dedication to the fulfilment of her calling, Millie demonstrates that to succeed in the journey of life requires your best and your all.

Like many before her, she begins to understand that a person is immortal until their given purpose is complete.

The challenge this book brings to its readers is two-fold. What will **you** give your life for, and who will you allow to assist and guide you on the journey of life?

Like every good teacher, Millie provides us with the answer. She would surely say, "Commit your life to Jesus

Christ. Trust him and he will guide you and lead you."
Her answer and her life demonstrates the wisdom she
too has found on her journey.

Keri Jones
Ministries Without Borders

Preface

The purpose of writing my life story is first as a legacy to my family, to my brother Stanley and his wife Joan and also to his three sons: Stuart, Nicholas and Martyn and their wives and families.

The second reason, but by no means of secondary importance, is to give thanks to God for the way He has led me from my childhood until now. As I look back over the years, I am eternally grateful for the upbringing I had which enabled me to find Jesus Christ, the Son of the Living God, at an early age.

My relationship with Him has brought me through circumstances and experiences in different parts of the world which I would never have dreamed of nor coped with otherwise.

It is my one desire that not only my family but all who read these memoirs will find Jesus Christ for themselves. He is very much alive and in the business today of making people whole – body, soul and spirit – and to make life worthwhile and exciting. I certainly recommend Him to you!

In Appreciation

I have been so blessed to have had wonderful places to write these memoirs, both in Africa and here in England.

My sincere thanks go to Piet and Rosemary Combrink, Tom and Rosemary Hobson, Monika Botha and Esther Townsend, for their kind invitation to stay with them on their beautiful farmland in Africa. Thanks also to Harold and Mary Rea for the freedom of their home and garden in Kitwe and to Charlie Rea for the use of his parents' home in Mwinilunga. All were havens of peace and restfulness.

In the United Kingdom, Douglas and Jean Milne's delightful cottage in an area called Paradise on the east coast of Scotland became another haven to put pen to paper. The final chapters were written mainly in my own home and in one of the Lakewood Cottages belonging to Alex and Christine Sayer of Lancaster. I am truly grateful to all these people.

And there are others too, who have encouraged me along the way, typed up sections of the manuscript (special thanks to Michelle Scott), made suggestions here and there, and introduced me to Maurice Barratt of Manchester, who kindly published this book at very short notice. My warmest thanks to all these people.

Proud parents with Mildred – only a few weeks old

Dad and Mother with Mildred – 4 Years old

Chapter One

Early Years

On August 13th 1926 a baby girl came into the world in Netherfield Road Maternity Hospital, Nelson, Lancashire. Her parents, Thomas and Lily Pratt, had both been born before the turn of the century in 1898, Thomas being the elder by just six weeks. Now in their early twenties, they had married and set up home together.

Their backgrounds were very different. Thomas, as he was always called by his mother, was the eldest of seven children. John came next, then Walter, then twins - only one of whom survived, Edith – Ivy came next and finally Clifford. As the family increased, there were more mouths to feed and it was not surprising that at the age of eleven Thomas had to work part time in a cotton mill.

Nelson was known as a textile town and was one of a number of towns situated in the valleys of East Lancashire. They were notable for two reasons; one was the damp climate prevalent in that area because of the hills and abundance of rain: and the second reason was because of the number of streams and rivers used for the transporting of bales of cloth which came off the looms. Waterways were essential and with the building of the Manchester Ship Canal (opened in 1894) and the Leeds and Liverpool Canal the need was met until roads were built later for goods to be carried by trucks.

So it was that Thomas at an early age was introduced to life in a textile mill. But life was not easy for him nor for his mother, Theresa. His father, John Pratt, also worked in a cotton mill and was earning good money, but sadly he was a heavy drinker. He was often found in the pub after pay-day, drinking his way through his wages, whilst at home Theresa was struggling to feed six hungry children. Tom would be sent out to find his father and drag him home. He knew exactly where he would be – either in the Engineer Arms, a pub near his home, or in the Lord Nelson, a pub in the center of town. Time and time again after Tom had received his wages, his father would commandeer the money and head off to the pub.

Fortunately, his father's influence did not rub off on Tommy Pratt. What a way to live and what a lifestyle! He was a capable boy and eager to learn, and as he grew older he enrolled for evening classes - or night school as these classes were called – to learn all he could about natural fibres (cotton, wool and flax) then later man-made fibres such as nylon, rayon, terylene and viscose. He achieved his National and Higher National Examinations in Textiles and by this time he was far better qualified than many of his contemporaries.

From weaving, he rose to 'overlooking' the work of a number of weavers which was better pay and one day he hoped to be a mill manager! By this time, he was one of the highest qualified persons in his field. But promotion always seemed to elude him. Whenever a position in management became available, it was always given to someone else, often less capable or less qualified than himself. The reason was this: he was not a drinker. He was not one of the boys! In the end he approached the owners of the mill and so it was that a post was created for him. It was arranged that in future every new employee would have to take a course of training starting with the spinning of the thread to the final results of woven material off the loom. It was an ideal post for Thomas. He loved it and became a very good teacher. He knew his subject well and was able to communicate knowledge to the students of his classes. Now he was on a better salary and no longer did he need to wear overalls to grovel under looms in need of repair. He was in a 'white-collar' job!

But Tom had other interests too. He had joined the local branch of the Salvation Army simply because it had a brass band! He was given a trumpet first, then a trombone and later a euphonium to master and he became a keen band member. Later he was to become the Junior Band Master because of his tenacity and capabilities. But not only that, through the Biblical teaching he received whilst attending the Salvation Army and through the influence of the life and example of William Booth, its founder, he realised his need of forgiveness for his sins in order to belong to a much greater Army – the Army of God. Thus it was in his mid-teens he made his way to the 'penitent form' at the front of the Hall known as the Citadel and asked Jesus Christ to make him clean and to accept him into His Kingdom. This was later to lead him into a deeper commitment of his life to God by the way of holiness, much emphasised by their teaching at that time.

Two years later Tom was sent to France to serve in the British Army of the 1914-1918 war. He was away the last two years of the war and during that time he carried with him a pocket New Testament inside of which was the Salvation Army crest. He also carried a small copy of 'Green Pastures' a little book of daily readings, given to him by his Sunday School teacher, Mrs John Townsley. These he carried with him in the top pocket of his tunic.

Years later he told me that everywhere he went there was a constant 'Presence' with him on his left shoulder. He had only to turn his head in that direction to feel tremendous comfort and strength as he faced each new danger in those fearful trenches of mud, stench and disease in France.

My mother's upbringing was very different. Her name was Eva Graham and she was born in Skipton, Yorkshire. Sadly, her mother died when she was three years of age and as her father, Dick Graham, had five children, three boys and two girls, and was unable to care for them, they were all brought up by various members of the Graham family, all except Annie. Annie stayed with her father until she married Billy Dickinson. Then they took Dad to live with them in Bingley, Yorkshire. Jack, her eldest brother, married a local girl, Esther, and they went to live in Hebden Bridge, also in Yorkshire. Harry married Ethel and they had three children, Evelyn, Jack and Harry junior. They lived at Saltaire, near Bradford. The youngest brother, Billy Graham, went to live in America – no relation to the famous evangelist of that name!

Eva was taken into the home of an uncle called Oswald Graham but as they already had a daughter called Eva, her name was changed to Lily, at her own request. Oswald and Mary Jane, his wife, lived in Nelson in a large house on the main road linking Colne with Nelson. They were keen worshippers of God and attended the Salvation Army in Nelson. Prior to her marriage to Oswald, Mary Jane had been a Salvation Army officer in Ireland. She was his second wife.

So it was that at an early age Mother was brought up to live with this family and her cousins Ernest, Maggie and Eva. Oswald was a lover of music and played the double bass, and every member of the family had to learn to play an instrument. Mother chose the violin, a very difficult instrument to play, as I discovered later!

As mother grew up in that household, she also enjoyed the activities of the Army and became a member of the 'Songsters', as the women of the choir were called. It was there that she met my father, as he was also musical and was a keen bandsman.

When father was called up to fight in France it was to be a very harrowing time for them both. Their friendship had blossomed and their parting was agony. But after two years Dad returned without injury and took up his former employment in the mill.

Much of the population worked in the local mills. The people worked hard. The days were long but the pay was good. On their feet they wore clogs with thick wooden soles and leather uppers. On the base of the soles were 'irons', strips of metal nailed round the edge to protect the wood and give longer life to the clog. But the racket they made when a vast number of people were on their way to work early in the morning and again at the end of the day, was unbelievable!

After the war, life continued as before for Tom and Lily but circumstances in both families brought about an early marriage. My father's hard-earned money being spent on his father's ale and mother being treated as a servant, having daily to scrub the paving stones of the scullery and kitchen floors after a hard day's work at the mill, made them decide to marry and have a home of their own. They were now in their early twenties and earning steady wages.

Their marriage took place at the Salvation Army and they set up home in a small terraced house in Belgrave Street, Nelson. It had four rooms, a kitchen and living room downstairs and two bedrooms upstairs. There was no bathroom as such but a bath and washbasin were installed in the back bedroom. This small terraced house in the middle of a row of granite houses had a small garden at the front and a yard at the back. Most gardens had railings round them but theirs had a low wall, on top of which were large white crystallised stones which glistened in the sun. I think these must have come from my grandfather as he had a large yard at the rear of his house with similar stones on a high wall.

It was into this setting that I came into the world in 1926. It was to be another seven years before my brother Stanley was born. I was named 'Mildred' after a favourite character of my mother's, a woman of noble birth called Mildred Duff who gave up a life of ease and the splendour of society to work among the youth of India. Mildred Duff died just six years after I was born, at the age of sixty-six.

Stanley was named after Stanley who was sent to find David Livingstone the geographical explorer in Africa. My brother was also given a middle name of Graham, mother's maiden name.

Our home was a humble home in many ways but with added refinements. We were the proud possessors of a piano, in ebony too! My father spent much of his spare time writing music and to possess a piano was a great asset. He would try out his chords and keys as he composed music for the band to play and later for the various choirs he would conduct. One piece he composed was called 'My Pathway'. He sent it to a publisher to be published which it was and it came back in a large, double-page format with an impressive title on the cover, which was edged with a blue border and had an inscription: 'Words and music by Thomas Pratt'. But it never took off. Technically it conformed to all the rules and regulations of written music but it was not the type of music that was popular in those days. It was not what people wanted. He was asked to write dance music, which he could very well have written, but he refused. He desired his talent to be used solely "for the service of God". To him, dance halls meant 'bars' - bars meant 'drink' and drink meant ruined homes.

But Dad certainly used his musical ability to the full. Not only could he play several brass instruments, he composed his own pieces, both words and music for the choir to sing when he became choir master. Each member of the family too had hymns dedicated to them.

But there was another piece of furniture which had pride of place in our living room - a mahogany sideboard. It was huge with a large mirror across the back, framed at the sides by two circular pillars which stood at each end of the surface. It was highly polished and had six drawers, the fronts of which were bevelled. This piece of furniture, along with the piano, were my parents' prized possessions. There was not another home in the street with such furniture. Mother had good taste and knew what she wanted and Father would carefully put money aside until they had the required amount to buy. Nothing was ever purchased on the 'never, never' as higher purchase was called. They saved up before they bought.

But to return to the rest of the furniture in the living room. A table in the middle of the room seated four people but could be extended by a panel in the centre, to seat eight. It was covered by a plush tablecloth, as it was always called. It was actually of a velour fabric and had a huge peacock on it with its tail fully outspread. The blue and green markings on the tail and head were spectacular. This was always covered with a white tablecloth when we had our meals. Four dining chairs and two armchairs completed the room. Entrance into this room was by the front door which had a vestibule across the corner. The upper half was made up of tiny panes of coloured glass held in place by strips of lead. These panes were known as leaded lights. The window was a sash window where both lower and upper parts could be opened by cords in the side frames. The upper part also had a design of coloured glass of red and green shapes joined together by thin leaded strips.

Our source of heating was by a coal fire which usually burned brightly in a low grate in the living room. The grate was flanked by green tiles embellished with a floral panel on either side. A copper canopy over the fire enabled the smoke to go up the chimney except on very windy days when gusts of wind would blow it into the room!

The kitchen also had a fire grate but was only used in exceptionally cold weather. Coal was stored in a shed in the back yard and two or three bags of coal were delivered each time by the coalman, whose face was as black as the product he sold from the dust which seeped through the sacks. Large pieces of coal were called 'cobs' and smaller ones were called 'nuts'. A fire was always made first with nuts and later cobs were added to keep the fire burning. Good coal burned well with very little residue of ash; poor coal would leave lumps of slate and stone among the dying embers. Ashes were collected in a shallow pan beneath the grate. Sometimes in the winter when it was extremely cold, a brick was paced at each side of the grate. As the fire burned these bricks would get very hot and would retain the heat for hours. We, as a family, would all sit round the fire, toasting our toes and enjoying the warmth.

Bags of coal were delivered on a handcart drawn by a horse. Each bag was carried on the back of the coalman to the various houses and dropped into the coal shed which was in the yard. Ashes were disposed of by carrying them from the house in a bucket and them dropped into an ash pit which was a deep hole in the wall, the base of which was at street level. A huge metal door kept them from spilling into the street. On collecting days they were removed from the pit and shovelled on to the cart, clouds of ash filling the air. The clanging of the doors opening and shutting, the clattering of the hooves of the horses on the cobbled street and the shouts of the men as they called to each other was a cacophony of sound I shall never forget. And this was a way of life until dustbins appeared! One thing was for sure, no washing was hung out on the street to dry on that day!

But to sit round the fireside in the evenings after our meal together, a day's work done, relaxing in the glow of the embers and sharing the happenings of our day with each other are truly treasured memories which will long remain with me.

Chapter Two

Growing Up

School days for me began when I was four years of age. I still remember the huge rocking horse in the corner of the classroom. We took turns to have a ride on it and extra rides were special treats when we had done something well. It was in this class that I was taught the alphabet and how to build up simple words. Addition and subtraction were mastered by using a bag of marbles!

But much of my time at primary school was clouded by ill health. Every childish ailment I seemed to 'catch': chickenpox, measles, whooping cough, even scarlet fever and in the winter time bronchitis and frequent colds and coughs. Once after a bout of German measles I had pneumonia. Doctors' visits had to be paid for in those days and much of my father's hard-earned money was spent on doctors' bills and medicines. Non-attendance at school, however, had its compensations. The bedroom became a place of comfort with a fire burning in the grate spreading a cosy glow throughout the darkened room in the evenings. My younger brother, Stanley, and I were blessed to have a caring mother. She was always there for us to nurse us through our illnesses. She never went out to work. Her place was in the home. Mother sent us off to school each day and was always there for us on our return home. Once when I had scarlet fever I lived in complete isolation in the bedroom away from the rest of the family and friends for six weeks. Mother was the only person I saw during that time as she attended to my daily needs. The room became bleak and bare as everything had to be burned after my recovery. Toys and books were limited as they had to be destroyed and favourite pictures had to be removed from the walls. After this ordeal the room had to be fumigated before life returned to normality.

All this changed, however, when I was sent to a special school for delicate children. We called it the Open Air School. It was situated in a delightful spot on the edge of town among the hills. The classroom blocks were surrounded by flower beds and each class was responsible for its own garden. Much of our time was spent outdoors and the whole atmosphere was relaxed and welcoming. We were given three nourishing meals each day, starting with breakfast on arrival in the morning and everything had to be eaten whether we liked it or not! We were not allowed to leave the table until our plates were clean. The school did not focus on examinations and consequently I missed a vital year prior to entry into grammar school. But it was the turning point of my life and when I entered grammar school the frail little girl had disappeared and a child with sturdy legs and arms emerged.

At that time we attended the Central Gospel Mission in Nelson. It was a large, impressive redbrick building with a garden of trees and shrubs. It was founded by a Scottish evangelist, David Ramsey and his wife. David was well-known for his artistic ability and drew good congregations by illustrating his talks with the paint brush as he preached.

Whilst attending this church something happened which was to change my whole life. A number of young people would meet prior to the Sunday morning service. Their ages were from nine to thirteen and they came to pray!! I joined them as I was into most things and was amazed to find that these children were praying to someone they appeared to know! I was saying prayers, words I had been taught by my parents. These children had no religious background whatsoever and yet they talked so easily and freely to some living, invisible person they really believed was there. It was an eye-opener to me and I felt out of my depth with them. As the weeks slipped by there was a growing uneasiness within me, until one Sunday the leader of the group, a dear lady called Muriel Shanley, invited us to open up our lives to Jesus Christ and to ask Him to come and reside within us by His Spirit. I knew I had never done that, I knew many things about Jesus but I did not know Him in a personal way. So I did just that and as I did so there came over me a tremendous sense of relief and release. I had obviously been under a deep conviction for some time that things were not right and I was depending on the faith of my parents to see me into the Kingdom of God. It had taken a few children in the neighbourhood, with no Christian background whatsoever, to open my eyes to the reality that Jesus Christ was a living person who could and would reside in me if I sincerely invited Him to do so. At this stage I had no sense of guilt or sin or a need for forgiveness. All I was aware of was that it was my faith and my invitation that gave Him the right of access into my life. But it was because of His love for me that He died on the cross to make this possible. Strangely I found it hard to tell my mother what I had done and it took several weeks before I could pluck up courage to tell her. I needn't have worried. She was overjoyed and said that she had prayed so much for this to happen. But there was more to follow. During the next few years I became fully involved in the life of the church and enjoyed every minute of it.

Sunday became one of the busiest days of the week. We were brought up to go to the Mission three times each Sunday. First, a full morning when the young people met for prayer at 9:30am before the main service, then home for lunch; back again in the afternoon for Sunday School, followed by the Sunshine Band – a group of women who went out in twos taking flowers to those who were ill or were infirm and unable to get out at all. This group often sang and prayed with these folks to give comfort and encouragement; home for tea and back again in the evening to attend an open air meeting followed by the evening gospel service. What a day! Of course we didn't attend everything, but there was plenty to choose from and the day was full. Some of the young people even met after the service for their Youth hour. And this was a day of rest!

At one time, four of us, together with three others, from another church, formed a team and went around singing and giving testimony to various other youth groups and churches in the area. We were a close-harmony trio (Joan Partridge, Margaret Emmot and myself) and a quartet (Derek Brierley and John Burgess) and did most of our practising on Sunday evenings after church. Our venue was the home of one of the girls, Margaret, who played the piano for us and was our main singer. These were evenings of great fun and hilarity as well as serious practice and the evenings usually ended with cups of tea and home-made cake served by the lady of the house who put up with so much of our chatter and banter! They were great days and enjoyed immensely by us all.

Joan, Margaret and Myself – The Singing Trio

At Margarets Ruby Wedding – 50 Years on

Pratt family – Dad second from left, top row

Leading Junior Band – Salvation Army
Dad – center

Chapter Three

Grandparents

A visit to my grandparents' home was a special treat. To me as a child, their home appeared rather grand. Their terraced garden was on a very steep slope flanked by a flight of stone steps which led from the gate to the front door. I remember as a child of seven, standing on those steps with my mother and grandparents, with my brother Stanley as a baby in Mother's arms, waiting to see King George V and Queen Mary as they travelled in a horse-drawn carriage through the town whilst visiting our area.

In the summer time the garden was a mass of bloom. Colourful clumps of blue lobelia and white rock were planted between huge stones and later red geraniums were added to the scene. It was always the same, year after year.

Inside the house a passage led from the front door to the foot of the stairs. The parlour, or sitting room, was on the left of the passage and was very rarely used. It contained very expensive, lacquered furniture, shiny blue-black, and the cupboards in the sideboard had pictures with ivory figures on the panels. On a sunny day, as the sun's rays shone through the big bay window, the whole room was filled with warmth and light. It was a special treat to be allowed to sit on one of the rugs scattered over the floor and read or play with my toys.

The next room, at the rear of the house, was always a hive of activity. Here my grandparents spent most of their time for this was their work room. They ran a knitting business from their home, mainly men's knee socks with fair isle tops. But they also knitted pullovers and cardigans or sweaters known as ganseys! They possessed two machines, one was a flat one which grandfather used mainly for his pullovers and sweaters, the other was a circular one which was used to knit stockings. Woollen ones were very popular and boys would often wear them with intricate fair isle patterns round the tops. It was fascinating to watch a tubular stocking emerge from below a circular machine as the handle was turned. When the required length had been reached, grandmother would hook all the stitches on to knitting needles and 'turn the heel by hand'. Then back to the machine again to complete the required length of foot and taper the toe. They would also repair worn-out stocking feet by cutting them off by the ankle and replacing them with new feet. In those days it was a common thing to have woollens stockings refooted when the heels and toes were worn out! To advertise their industry we had a sign in our window at home. It read:

"Stockings knitted or refooted
ribbed or plain"

People could also bring their own wool and have garments knitted to their own requirements.

At such times when I visited them as a child, mainly with my mother, my grandfather would be bent over his machine near the window in order to obtain as much light as possible. His white hair in a curly tuft on the top of his head and his rosy cheeks were a familiar sight. Always cheerful, always busy and if not at his work, he would be in his greenhouse in the yard at the back of the house during the week. Sunday, however, was a day of rest. Covers were placed over the machines, business stopped and everyone went off to the Salvation Army, dressed in their Sunday best.

Evidence of my grandmother's past life as a Salvation Army officer was in abundance in that work room also. There was a huge sideboard of mahogany wood which my grandfather had had made. It was a beautiful piece of furniture with elegant carvings of fruit and leaves on the drawers and cupboards. On the surface, numerous white china ornaments were displayed, each bearing the coat of arms of a town or city in the British Isles. Prior to her marriage to granddad, my grandmother had travelled widely as a Salvation Army officer and consequently had an enormous collection of these china ornaments. They were very special and covered the entire surface. There were bicycles, post vans, cars, pillar boxes, shops, people – just about everything and they had pride of place in that home.

Grandmother, who was quite a buxom person, would sit by the fireside, a bright fire burning in a big, black fire range with ovens on each side, her knitting needles clicking speedily when she was not working on a machine. Dough would be rising in a large basin covered with a cloth, near the fire. When it had filled the basin, it would be kneaded well and returned to a warm place to rise again before being put into loaf tins and popped into the ovens to bake delicious loaves of bread.

In later years when dusting became too big a chore, these china ornaments were put into a large box and designated to the attic. From time to time, I was allowed to climb the stairs to the top of the house and set out these precious objects as a village and I spent endless hours of enjoyment in that attic.

One other thing must be mentioned. A grandfather clock stood tall across the corner of the room next to the mahogany sideboard. On its face, above the hands, a moon would appear peeping over billowy clouds. Each phase from a thin sliver of a new moon to a complete round face of a full moon fascinated us as we compared it with the moon in the sky outside. We never saw the moon move on the clock but it was always accurate when we were able to see the moon outside on a clear night, whatever the phase might be.

We used to sing a song about a grandfather's clock:

" My grandfather's clock was too big for the shelf
So it stood by itself on the floor
It wasn't half as tall as the old man himself
And it didn't weigh a penny weight more
It was bought on the morn of the day that he
was born
It was always his pleasure and pride
But it stopped short, never to go again
When the old man died

CHORUS:

Ninety years without slumbering, tick tock, tick
tock

Life's moments numbering, tick tock, tick tock
But it stopped, short, never to go again
When the old man died!"

After my grandfather's death, eventually the big house was sold and Grandma went to live in a small terraced house which she shared with her sister who was also a widow. They each had a bedroom and their own living room and lived independently of each other, in the village of Barrowford near Nelson. Unfortunately the house was situated near a river and several times after torrential rains the river would overflow its banks and pour down the streets into the house, causing terrible devastation. Carpets and furniture would be floating on the water which often rose to well over a foot deep in the downstairs rooms. The drains were not big enough to take large quantities of water and after the water had subsided, carpets caked with mud had to be cleaned and furniture restored and often re-polished.

Several years later, after qualifying as a teacher, my first post was in that village and I became a frequent visitor there. Through those visits I learned of her extreme generosity. Whatever one took her in the way of gifts, be it fruit, flowers or groceries, she would always pass them on to others whose needs were greater than her own. The only way we could really bless her was to decorate her rooms or give her items of furniture which were too heavy for her to pass on to others!

One last memory which will always remain with me was of her final moments on this earth. Dad was sitting by her bedside and they were having a conversation as though she was going on an outing the following day and would be seeing my mother, who incidentally had died some years earlier! The conversation ran something like this: "Tell Lily we are all getting on fine. Stanley is now in college and doing well and Mildred is still enjoying teaching at Barrowford. Give her our love and tell her it won't be too long before we shall see her again."

I stood there transfixed, tears streaming down my face as I listened. It was not only the fact of having lost my mother, and I was about to lose my grandmother too, but also that Dad really believed there was life after death and that we would truly see those dear to us again if we had the faith to believe and trust in Jesus in this life. Death was like a gateway into a life beyond where there would be no more pain and suffering, heartache or sadness.

I have pictured this scene many times since and realise now that my own beliefs were strengthened through that conversation, that death is not the end but entrance into a new life beyond.

The story of my paternal grandparents is very different. I never knew Granddad Pratt. He died at an early age but Grandma lived on into her seventies. She was a tiny person and to me always looked thin and careworn until her children married and left home. Only one daughter, Edith, remained single in her lifetime and she looked after Grandma until her death.

They had one ambition and that was to leave the town of Nelson with its mills, cobbled streets and clogs and move to the seaside, Blackpool being their preference. The day came when they bought a little house in Marton near Blackpool and settled there. They both loved the sunshine and were outdoors as often as possible. Soon they were both as brown as berries and they loved it. Edith took seasonal work on the pleasure beach and amusement arcades, where again she worked mainly outdoors. As children, my cousin Derek from Morecambe and I had a great time when we visited them and were given free rides on the Waltzer and the Big Wheel and Dobby Horses! Edith also did a stint in Morecambe one or two seasons and that was an added bonus. We were given a handful of 'dud' coins for the slot machines and of course if we won anything, the reward was in 'dud' coins! We reaped what we sowed. We would try our skill in manoeuvring a clutching hand hovering over a number of tempting objects such as pen and pencil sets, wrist watches and the like, mingled with 'jammy dodger' biscuits in little packs.

But all to no avail. Every single item would slip through its fingers as it swung over the exit hole, only to deposit an aniseed ball into the cup below, much to our disappointment.

In her later years, Grandma Pratt began to attend a Gospel Mission close to her home and I firmly believe she had a personal encounter with Jesus Christ before she died. Her daughter too, Auntie Edith, after the death of her husband John Fadden, told me of her experience of committing her life to God and thanking Him for the resurrection of Jesus, that He was no longer dead but very much alive. As she clutched a little gold cross on a wooden base which she kept on the fireplace, she repeated over and over, "It is not this, it is the person who was on it."

It was a wonderful thing for my father to know that his mother had been 'born again' into the Kingdom of God. His prayers had been answered and for his sister, too, though at that time she had yet to experience the forgiveness of God. But her time came and she never looked back.

Mother and Grandparents at Nelson

Dad, Stanley and myself without Mum – 1950

Chapter Four
Salad Days

A time of youthful inexperience

Throughout our lives choices have to be made, important decisions which so often affect the rest of our days. Such was the case for me when choosing a career. My father wanted me to train as a teacher, a career he would dearly have wished for himself but was never given the opportunity in his younger days. Later in life, however, he was to achieve his ambition in a unique way.

Teaching was not my first choice but when an opportunity came to train as a General Science teacher with Biology as a main subject, I readily accepted, especially as I would be based in Keswick in the Lake District, one of the most delightful spots in the country.

I was seventeen at the time – September1944 – and a new phase in my life was about to begin. I went off to St. Katharine's College and loved every minute of my student days there. The College had been relocated from Liverpool to Keswick during the war years. Most of our lectures were in the Queens Hotel in the main street and the students occupied various beautiful houses in their own grounds around the district. This meant a certain amount of freedom which we would not have had otherwise. We travelled around on bicycles to our lectures and it was a common sight to see young ladies with their purple blazers and pin-striped blouses, grey skirts and knee socks thronging the streets. We met together for our meals at Waverley Café, a restaurant in the centre of town, next to the Post Office, where the college occupied the whole building.

We were not allowed home at weekend and special days' holidays, but this gave wonderful opportunities to climb the hills and fells, to swim in the streams and to row on the lakes. For me, these were halcyon days and I even achieved my goal of scaling the peaks of Scafell, Striding Edge of Helvellyn, Skiddaw and the Gables and to prove it my little legs grew sturdier and more muscular with each climb!

Term-time began late September when the landscape was changing from its lush, verdant pastures to brilliant shades of amber, gold, bronze and russet as the leaves of the trees put on their autumn garments. But on returning home for the Christmas holidays, often the scene had totally changed. Sometimes a thick, white mantle lay on the ground and the hills and snow-capped peaks would sparkle in the sun. Their streams, no longer cascading down the mountainside, lay sparkling, frozen stiff in the cold, icy blast of the winter's wind. Then spring would be upon us once more, snow and ice gone and from the ground snowdrops would first make their appearance, followed by primroses and primulas, crocuses and polyanthas everywhere. But when fields and hedgerows were filled with daffodils, then we knew that spring had certainly arrived! Every season had its own beauty and the journey from Preston to Keswick on the train, crossing the River Greta several times, was spectacular.

It was whilst I was at College that news came to us that a certain Major Ian Thomas had taken possession of a country mansion, Capernwray Hall near Carnforth in north Lancashire. He and his wife, Joan, together with Major Greenwood and his wife, were to run this place as a Holiday Conference Centre for young people. The following year my friends and I booked in for a holiday there, which certainly turned out to be a holiday with a difference.

It was there that I learned through Ian Thomas's own amazing life story what God could do with a life totally surrendered and committed to Him in every area – time, money, career, recreation, friendships, marriage – everything! I learned that God had a plan for everyone's life, including me! He knew the day I was born, He knows the day I will die. To place my life into His hands would, to use Ian's own words, "no longer be my responsibility but my response to His ability". I would be energised and motivated by the Holy Spirit as I made myself available to God each day.

This was a new concept to me. I had no doubts about believing I was a Christian but to get on to God's wavelength and to allow Him to fulfil the purpose for which I was created was entirely new. Whatever God had called me to do, He would equip and show me every step of the way. Just one thing was necessary. I would need to spend time in God's presence, regularly feeding on His Word, the Bible, learning to listen to His voice and then put into practice the instructions He had given me, "Being told what to do and doing what you are told", said Ian. I wanted this with all my heart and although it was easier said than done, I promised God I would do whatever He wanted me to do and go wherever He wanted to send me. The sky was the limit and I really meant it.

Two years later I left college with excellent results, a pair of sturdy legs and an invitation to stay on another year to do research work on seaweed! I had loved every minute of my time in the Lake District and to stay on another year would have been an added bonus. But it was not to be.

Meanwhile, at home changes were taking place. We no longer lived in a little terraced house. Our home was now a semi-detached dwelling on a hill overlooking a lovely park with a swimming pool. We had a large garden and Stanley and I revelled in spending days outdoors enjoying the long, warm summer evenings. Stanley was very fond of pets and at one time or another had various rabbits, a Belgian hare and a cat called Topsy. From school he went to a commercial college and after graduating was appointed to a post in the local council offices in Brierfield in Lancashire, starting first as 'tea-boy' and eventually finishing as the Borough Surveyor or Public Health Inspector (as the post later became known) for the same council.

One day Stanley came home to discover Mother had collapsed on the floor in a pool of blood. Investigations followed and the results revealed cancer of the rectum. This meant a colostomy, not a common thing in those days. Would she be able to cope with the operation as she had a very weak heart? At this time I was half-way through my course at College. Should I continue or should I return home? Mum said "Come", Dad said "Stay and finish your course". Mum survived the operation and I finished my course but not without much heartache. It was 'touch and go' whether she would survive the next two years. She actually lived for eighteen months.

One Saturday Mum and Dad went on an outing in the country with the church choir. A very heavy downpour of rain caused everyone to run for shelter. That evening Mum had a massive heart attack and died during the night. She was forty seven years of age. This was a tremendous shock to us all. Our lives would never be the same and instantly I knew that my place was to be at home with the family. It also meant that I needed to obtain a post nearby. Normally students were sent to city schools to do a probationary year which was to be part of their final exam. I obtained a post at a senior, co-educational central school in the nearby village of Barrowford. The only post that could be offered to me was to teach Art and History throughout the school. My heart sank to the depths of my boots. Out of ten subjects at matriculation level the only one I had failed was Art and I had been bored to tears with History – all dates and battles – that I had dropped the subject as soon as I could. Here I was, newly qualified, teaching subjects that I knew nothing about, and the added burden of running the household for my father and brother aged thirteen years. I felt absolutely trapped, but trapped on the promises of God! In one aspect it was the hardest year of my life and my one aim was to get the year over and apply for another post elsewhere.

But God had other plans. The school was an excellent one under the headship of Kenneth Sharp, who was very firm but kindly. I learned so much from him. Discipline was good, standards were high and I could not have had a better foundation for teaching. Above all I had Someone on whom I could draw the necessary wisdom and strength which I so needed and He was only a prayer away!

My aim was to encourage everyone to have some work on display on the walls of my spacious light art room where I was privileged to work. All too often attention is only given to a favoured few who have a flair for drawing. This was not so in my case. Attending short courses had given me lots of ideas and eventually History and Art became a delight to teach. Everyone was involved in depicting social life in England throughout the ages, on a time chart which stretched around the room. This linked not only each individual's work but each year's work. Absence of pressure to pass exams gave freedom for expression in many different ways and often History and Art were correlated. Consequently, the desire to leave after one year stretched to ten! Sadly, at the end of that time, the headmaster died of cancer at the age of 54 and, as my father had remarried, it was the right time to move on.

Ian and Joan Thomas with Christopher,
Mark and Peter – Andrew not yet born

Chapter Five
Southport

Every year Dad made sure we had a family holiday, usually in one of the coastal towns of Lancashire. Blackpool was a favourite as Grandma lived there with an unmarried daughter, Edith, who was great fun to be with. But Dad had a brother in Morecambe and sometimes our annual holiday was spent with the family there.

Southport was another coastal town with beautiful golden sand stretching for miles. Unfortunately, the sea always appeared to be miles out and it was a rare occasion to see the waves breaking against the pier, known to be the third longest pier in England.

Southport was also noted for its famous Lord Street, a long tree-lined road with beautiful high-class shops under their glass canopy on one side and gardens on the other. Many holiday makers came here because the climate was warmer and there was an air of splendour about the resort.

Southport was to be my next home. An Art teaching post became available at a large girls' school there, which I accepted. But after three years at Meols Cop School I was surprised to be asked to establish and head up a new Religious Education department up to 'O' level standard. Yet again, no qualifications in this area but by this time I was an experienced teacher. What an opportunity to present the story of Jesus as portrayed in the Gospels and the Acts of the Apostles! This was straight teaching of the Bible text. The Scriptures would speak for themselves and they certainly did!

Religious Education was often looked upon as a 'Cinderella' subject. My task was to take away that image and give it its rightful place on any school curriculum. To me it was a living subject and my aim would be to encourage students to enjoy it so much that they would approach the Bible with different eyes and read it for themselves. After all, didn't I believe the Bible to be God's Word to all mankind and in it I had found the answer to many puzzling problems? What's more, didn't I believe that Jesus was not some historical person long-since dead? He is the Son of God. He rose again and is alive today. Furthermore, didn't I believe that He was living within me, by His Spirit, to enable me to become the person He wanted me to be and to fulfil the purpose for which I was created? It was indeed a tremendous opportunity to head up the department and I grasped it with both hands.

Shortly after my arrival, I was introduced to a member of staff, Dorothy Barton, who I discovered was a Christian. A firm friendship evolved which was to last throughout the years. Later we ran a Scripture Union group together after school hours and met daily to pray for girls who were in that group.

The Bible can be a very off-putting book to read – small print, archaic language, long names of the various books of which it is made up. But today modern versions and translations in good size print with attractive covers have made it much more approachable. As a subject in school, attractive ways had to be found to introduce this library of books. Sixty-six books with over forty authors, divided into two sections, the Old and New Testaments, prompted the idea of matchbox libraries. Pupils were encouraged to collect matchboxes of the same size and to turn them on end with the rough side acting as the spine of the book. A name of one book of the Bible was printed neatly on each spine and so the whole collection was built up in this way. Then they had to be assembled in some form of 'bookcase' to keep them together. Shoe boxes were the most common way, but then parents became involved and soon miniature wooden bookcases appeared, or cardboard models from cereal boxes. Others really excelled by completing the ensemble with mantle clocks and ornaments. All this was homework of course and such fun. At open days I was introduced to a number of parents who had been involved in the model-making and were also able to quote the books of the Bible!

Most Heads of Department were asked to write a syllabus for their own subject. Again this gave a wonderful opportunity to introduce Christian biography, especially with classes not under pressure to take exams. It usually worked out a term of New Testament, one of Old Testament and a third reading a Christian biography.

Gladys Aylward's life was a favourite from the book 'The Small Woman' by Alan Burgess. It is an amazing story of God's call on a small, insignificant young woman living in east London to go to China to work for Him there. She had no training and nothing to offer, but one thing she knew: God had called her and she was determined to go. She offered herself to God with her total possessions of two and a half pence and her Bible! "Here is my Bible, here is my money and here is me. Find some way to use me God."

This story was high-lighted by the fact that Gladys visited England after some years in China and I was privileged to meet her and to invite her to the school. She brought with her a seven-year-old Chinese boy called Gordon. By this time also a film had been made of her life, 'The Inn Of The Sixth Happiness', which the pupils saw.

This story had a profound effect on one of the my pupils, Miriam. Sadly, Miriam was killed in a road accident when riding to school one day on her bicycle. She was thirteen years of age. Her mother told me later how impressed she had been by the story of Gladys Aylward and Miriam too had said, "Here is my Bible, here is my money. Use me God." The family mourned for their lovely daughter but they had an inner peace knowing that she was safe with her Lord and Master, whom she had so desired to serve.

Gladys Aylward gave me a white silk banner with the inscription 'Aylward House' in red felt Chinese characters and also written in English. This had been hung outside the orphanage which she had founded, after rescuing a hundred children from the Japanese soldiers when China was at war with Japan. This was probably in Formosa, now Taiwan, when she was unable to go back into China.

But to return back to the syllabus! Another book which gripped the pupils was 'Pilgrim's Progress' by John Bunyan. This had always been heavy reading for me as a child but it is a superb allegory of a Christian's journey from the City of Destruction to the Celestial City. The teaching of this came alive with a chart around the room of a road linking the two cities. It passed through the countryside, arriving at such places as the Slough of Despond, Doubting Castle and Vanity Fair. It also depicted some of the characters that Christian (the hero) met on his way – Evangelist, Mr Worldly Wiseman, Giant Despair, Faithful and Hopeful – until he came to the river which had to be crossed before he could enter the Celestial City. It was a good story and it gave ample opportunity to compare situations in everyday life.

Another ten years passed by, during which time I had found a spiritual 'home' at Bethesda Chapel. I had visited a number of churches in the town but eventually was drawn to Bethesda because of the warm welcome I always received and the large number of young people there. Also, I had found a good friend in Dorothy Taylor (nee Barton), who not only taught at the same school but attended Bethesda Chapel. Eventually we were involved together with a number of youth activities which included membership into the Girl Covenanter movement, Merseyside Youth Camps in the summer, and joint events with the Boy Covenanter Group which commenced around the same time.

The same year that I had arrived in Southport, two families arrived from Manchester by the name of Whitehead: Herbert and Eveline with their two daughters Grace and Ruth and Norman and Beatrice with their daughters Helen and Sara. They had with them also Nana Whitehead, an unmarried brother Edward (Ted) and the mother of Eveline and Beatrice, as two brothers had married two sisters! Herbert became involved in the leadership of the Boy Covenanter Group, together with Jess Hindle and Norman Crompton.

Typical Zambian villlage scenes

Chapter Six
Zambia

Each year in Southport the International Revival Convention, led by Maynard James, drew people from many areas in Britain and the meetings were well attended and ran for a whole week. Friday evening was devoted to work abroad and missionaries from various parts of the world were given the opportunity to tell of their work and to emphasise the needs of their particular country. I had been to many such meetings and had never felt that God was calling me to serve Him abroad. I was in the unique position of teaching Bible Knowledge to senior students with emphasis on the Gospels and the Acts of the Apostles. The Scriptures often stimulated discussion both in the classroom and after school and this had proved to be a mission field in itself.

On this particular Friday evening, the speaker was Len Moules of Worldwide Evengelisation Crusade. He spoke of the wide open door in Africa for the spread of the Gospel – a day **of** youth and a day **for** youth. Seventy five per cent of the population in Africa were under twenty five years of age. Very few people lived above the age of forty at that time. He made a strong appeal for the youth to give themselves full-time to the service of Jesus Christ in Africa.

His verse was from Judges 4:14 –

"But this is the day, has not the Lord gone out
before you".

Immediately I knew within my heart that God was speaking to me and I was in shock! I sat down trembling, my face as white as a sheet. Could this be true? This was also confirmed in the scripture from the book of Jeremiah –

"You shall go to all I send you and whatsoever I
command you, you shall speak. Be not afraid of
their faces for I am with you".

But in all big decision-making, it is wise to put the issue to the test. For me this was a big move. What about my post at school? By this time I was heading up the Religious Education department at Meols Cop, giving me wonderful opportunities to speak about the Lord Jesus.

At church I was co-leader, with my friend Dorothy, of a Girl Covenanter group of teenage girls. Merseyside Youth Camps, which often took place in Wales, occupied much of our summer holidays. What is more, I had just furnished a flat which occupied part of a building next to the church, where youth activities were held each week. Could I just walk out and leave all this to live elsewhere?

So I asked God that if this calling to Africa was really for me, then I would be replaced by a Christian teacher. The headmistress also was keen to have a Christian to fill the post. I also asked God what I should do about my flat and its furniture.

God certainly answered my prayer and it all came about in this way. The flat beneath mine was occupied by an elderly couple from the church. One weekend, a visiting couple with their daughter Kath came to stay with them. I was introduced to Kath and was asked if I would entertain her for the weekend. To cut a long story short, I found out that she was to have been married but her fiancé had broken off the engagement at the last minute, which had caused her great distress. Kath was a Religious Education teacher and was seeking another post in another town to try to put her life back together again. She also belonged to the same church denomination as I did. So together we prayerfully committed the whole situation into God's hands and Kath applied for the post and got it! She not only took over the post but also joined the church and shared the leadership of the Girl Covenanter Group. She applied for my flat and this also was approved. Consequently, when I left for Africa, friends took my furniture, leaving me with crockery and cutlery for Zambia and Kath set up home in Southport with the wedding presents she had received. God had truly answered prayer in a remarkable way, not only confirming my call to Africa abut also giving Kath a new start.

One question still remained: where in Africa should I go? It was almost 12 months before that question was answered. Northern Rhodesia had gained its independence from Britain and had become known as Zambia from the name of the great River Zambezi, which flows through the country. About that time I was put in touch with an elderly missionary living in a remote bush area in that country. Her name was Hilda Kelly, formerly from Liverpool, and she was praying for a younger person to take her place. Hilda was a trained teacher and missionary and when President Kaunda came to power, he had set up secondary boarding schools in many remote areas in Zambia. Hilda seized the opportunity to teach the students when a school was built in Mwinilunga. Not only did she teach but she opened up a small bookshop for the sale of educational books, stationery, writing materials and Christian literature and Bibles in different tribal languages. But to teach and run a bookshop was too much for her. She was in urgent need of someone to take over the school work.

Consequently, when I wrote to her, I received a telegram: "Urgently needed, letter following." When the letter came it was written on toilet paper! And what a letter! This school was in a remote bush area, situated in the north-western corner of the country, almost on the Republic of Congo border and very close to Angola. It was three hundred miles to the nearest town, Chingola, on the Copper Belt and the road was hazardous. It was a dirt road, full of potholes, narrow in places, winding up hill and down ravines, crossing a number of rivers – over which there were very rickety bridges! Mwinilunga itself was a mere township with no gas, no electricity, no running water, no public transport – just a track with a few scattered houses on either side.

Such was the picture written on Jeyes toilet paper and I was under no illusion as to what I should find. But as I read all this, somehow I was not put off. There was a stirring in my spirit and the more I prayed about it, the more convinced I became that this was the place for me.

So it came about that in October 1967 I set sail on the 'Pendennis Castle' from Southampton with three other young missionaries – Mary Eastbury, Gwyneth Stormont and Gillian Harris. Gillian had a vehicle with her and the plan was to share the driving from Cape Town through the Karoo to Pretoria and Beitbridge then on to Livingstone, where we arrived on Independence Day (24th October 1964) at 8:00pm. We passed through immigration and customs without a hitch, for which we thanked God, for many had had trouble at this stage. Very few officers were on duty that night!

Next morning, on Zambian soil, our first task was to see the Eastern Cataract of the famous Victoria Falls, where, years earlier, David Livingstone had stood and named them after Queen Victoria. Little did I realise that years later I would be living in close proximity to these Falls.

It was an awesome sight to see water falling over a ledge a mile in length, into a deep gorge below. Further visits years later after rainy seasons made me realise why they were called 'The Smoke That Thunders!' (Mosi-o-Tunya). Torrents of water from the tributaries of the River Zambezi from the northern parts of the country thundered into the gorge, causing enormous spray high into the air which could be seen for miles around. Sometimes the spray was so dense that the water falling into the gorge could not be seen, and raincoats and umbrellas were absolutely essential. Much depended on the direction of the wind. On one occasion I was caught out and was thoroughly soaked to the skin, my dress clinging to me and my shoes squelching with water as we walked the mile across.

Our next main stop was in Luanshya on the Copper Belt. We were travelling during the hottest time of the year and the heat was appalling. I remember we were sitting on our towels to soak up the perspiration! We arrived at the home of Dr David and Mrs Roseannah Kay, who made us very welcome. Here we attended to the business of getting our national registration cards complete with photographs and a Zambian driving licence. Then the party separated and I went off with Darrell Rea on a 350 mile journey to Mwinilunga. And what a journey! Tarmac roads now left behind, we travelled at breathtaking speed in a Mercedes Benz on a dusty winding dirt 'road' of red earth and potholes. It was a night to be remembered and as we entered Bush country, from the thick forest of trees on either side, red eyes of the wildebeests gleamed at us like bicycle reflectors. The bush was full of sounds: crickets chirping, frogs croaking and strange birds calling. As we travelled through the night our way led over streams and rivers with rickety bridges and, to add to the excitement, we ran over a snake, a night-jar crashed into the windscreen (dazzled by the headlights) and a jackal met its doom as it shot in front of the car. But we finally arrived safe and sound in six hours flat!

The next few days were spent resting in the Reas' home, adapting to the colossal heat and a totally new lifestyle, before I was introduced to my senior missionary and to the life of the secondary boarding school.

Chapter Seven

Mwinilunga

meaning 'Head of the River Lunga'

Meeting Hilda Kelly was quite an experience. She was a teacher and missionary with a clear vision of what she wanted to achieve among the students at the secondary school and the people of Zambia generally. She was a woman of large proportion with a dogged determination to succeed. But she was a woman before her time. Much of what she strived for I was to see in the next sixteen years that I was there!

Strangely, when it became known that I was to come to Mwinilunga to relieve Hilda of the schoolwork, everyone imagined that I, too, would be a big strapping woman like she was! Imagine their surprise when I arrived, only five foot tall, tiny and slim, but with the same enthusiasm and drive that Hilda had.

Mwinilunga itself was a very small township along a dirt road, with a few small houses scattered on either side of the road. It did, however, boast of a tiny post office where mail was delivered once each week by bus, a police station, the beginnings of a hospital, a store and secondary school with staff houses – all without running water, gas or electricity!

My house was to be on the school compound and as a qualified British teacher, I was allowed the use of one of the staff houses in exchange for my services to the school. I was to teach Bible Knowledge to every class and the top three forms to 'O' level standard. This was very similar to the work I had been doing in England, the main difference being that Cambridge was the examining body and not Oxford as it was in England.

But the pressure was well and truly on. English was the students' second language and they were taught English in primary schools by qualified Zambian teachers! Pronunciation was appalling and sentence construction non-existent. Endless marking was necessary until, after five years of this, I could take no more!

By this time William and Eunice Rea had arrived as missionaries and they took over much of the teaching, leaving me with the examination classes until I left for Livingstone some years later. William took over those classes also after my departure.

Secondary schools throughout the country were staffed by expatriate teachers who came on two and a half year contracts from Britain, Canada and America. At the end of that time they could extend for another six months.

At that time a young couple, John and Julia Sutton-Smith, with their two children, David and Michael, were on contract at the school. John was teaching English and Physical Education. Prior to my arrival, John had become a Christian through the friendship and testimony of Darrell Rea, a local businessman. Darrell and Helen Rea not only ran a store in the township but also opened their home on Sunday evenings to the staff of the school. These were times of relaxation, listening to records, reading, discussion and buffet suppers. Many of the staff went just to be off the school compound, as the Reas lived four miles away at the top of a hill overlooking the Lunga River. They were good evenings and Darrell always closed with a reading from the Bible and threw out questions which were thought-provoking and stimulated discussion. Not only was Darrell a respected businessman but also a great hunter and fisherman. Animal heads of buffalo, reedbuck, waterbuck, duiker and many other African bush animals were to be seen on the walls of their sitting room.

When John and Julia's contract ended they extended it for another six months and it was during that time that Julia became a Christian at a fishing camp which Darrell organised.

Meanwhile, Hilda Kelly was getting on in years and failing in health. When an opportunity came for her to move to Luanshya, a Copper Belt town, to be in charge of a bookstore there, she gladly agreed, especially as the store was attached to the house where she would live. An avid reader herself, Hilda had done much to develop the spiritual life of John and Julia by encouraging them to read books of such authors as Tozer, Watchman Nee and C.S. Lewis. These were devoured eagerly as they themselves were avid readers. They also plied me with many questions about spiritual growth, guidance, knowing God's will, hearing His voice and knowing our enemy Satan.

At this stage, Ken and Ann Harper, who were missionaries at Kalene Mission Station fifty miles away, offered to take over the bookshop. This they did and employed a Zambian salesman, Solomon Kanswata, to run the shop whilst they made trips to the Copperbelt to buy stock for it.

Eventually they returned to England for their children's education, leaving Solomon in charge. I was asked to oversee the accounts whilst Solomon trained another salesman to remain in the shop, freeing him to do buying trips. He bought himself a motorbike and sent up his purchases on the bus – a three hundred mile journey!

There was also a big demand for stationery as the school grew in size. Exercise books, files, hard cover notebooks, pens and pencils were in constant demand and kept us busy. If we were able to buy pictures and posters with texts on or obtain Bible wallets and bags or T-shirts, all these things were an added bonus and brought in customers from far and wide.

As Mwinilunga Secondary School was a boarding school in a remote area, weekends and holidays were confined to the school compound. But the headmaster welcomed any supervised activities which would occupy the students over these periods. As Christians we took advantage of these times and organised a Youth Service on Sunday mornings at the local church. Students were allowed to go either to the Roman Catholic church or to the Brethren church which went under the name of Christian Missions of Many Lands (CMML), chosen by the missionaries for government purposes. This title covered a number of other countries also. These churches were packed each Sunday because it gave the students liberty to leave the school compound! Later, because their time was mis-used, services were held on the school premises, but were still well attended. Missionaries from the surrounding areas came to address CMML services and Catholic services were led by their own priests.

Gordon Suckling was a frequent visitor to the school. He and his wife Peggy were missionaries at Sachibondu River, twenty-two miles away. Formerly Gordon had been another great hunter and fisherman, a great friend of Darrell Rea's. But now Sachibondu had become a beautiful Retreat Centre and Bible school with its 'rondavels' (round huts with concrete floors and thatched roofs) scattered over the hillside. Not only did missionaries come from all over Zambia for times of rest and relaxation, Gordon and Peggy also organised Youth Camps for students at the secondary school. Dormitory accommodation was provided in different areas for boys and for girls and each camp had its own kitchens and dining room areas, again with concrete floors and thatched roofs held up on poles which created open sides to allow the breeze to come through. These Youth Camps were extremely popular and became a reaping ground for the Kingdom of God, as talks were given round the camp fires at night.

Back at school, after Camp was over, every endeavour was made to encourage Christian students to grow in their newly-found faith in Jesus Christ. Scripture Union was a very active organisation in Zambia and had produced a programme of daily Bible readings and notes to encourage practical Christian living. The notes were in a little booklet called 'Daily Power' and came out bi-monthly. We met in a classroom each morning at 6:30am to read God's Word and commit the day to Him. Many times the classroom was packed to capacity with 60-70 students. These times were led by John Sutton-Smith (who was now deputy head of the school), Brian Bentley or myself. Brian, who had joined the staff, was a qualified science teacher and son of Mr and Mrs Will Bentley, missionaries at Kamapanda, a mission station near the Angolan border. These early morning sessions were an inspiration to us all. It was such a joy to see the eagerness of those senior boys in particular whose ages ranged from 14-27 years! This was so because when education was offered to the youth of Zambia, there was no particular age limit into primary schools. Consequently, men of all ages, many of whom were married but claiming to be single, applied and were given entrance!

It was while teaching at Mwinilunga Secondary School that opportunity came to all heads of departments to compile a syllabus to 'O' level standard in their particular subject. Religious Education, as the subject was called, was mainly taught by Christian missionaries of various denominations. Ten of us met on the Copper Belt to discuss content. It was to be Bible-based with one term of Old Testament, one of New Testament and a third term of practical Christian witness and behaviour. It was to meet the requirements of the Zambia Examinations Council and also the approval of Cambridge University as the examining body.

As there were no libraries or reference books available to Zambian teachers, it was decided that a teachers' handbook would be necessary to encourage more teachers to teach Religious Education. Consequently, each term was planned with specific lessons on a theme, each with aims, teaching material, content, pupils' activities and assignments. Much work and research went into it, but on completion it was highly successful. Two thousand copies were printed in the first edition, believing that this was more than enough for the number of teachers presently teaching this subject. But it was so popular that ministers and clergymen were also buying it to preach from on Sundays! Even students were wanting to buy the handbook, so much so that it was decided a Pupil's Book for each grade should be written, too.

Rae Masterton of New Zealand, a missionary in Luanshya took on the responsibility of heading up this colossal task and did a magnificent job. Several of us did various sections but communication was almost impossible because we were scattered all over the country. Finally other missionaries from New Zealand joined Rae and the task was finally completed and put to the test in the schools nearby. This first edition was financed by the Brethren Assemblies in New Zealand and by Everday Publications Inc, Canada.

Since then another edition has been revised and produced with the Zambian government taking financial responsibility. The subject is still widely taught across the country and is a popular choice of an 'O' level subject because of available information and excellent exam results.

Hilda Kelly with Zambian women and children

This one didn't get away!
Fishing in the River Lunga

Chapter Eight
Problems

It was often said to me, "Why don't you leave these people alone? Why do you want to change their culture and customs?" Why indeed? I'll tell you why – because they live in constant fear. African people throughout the continent are very conscious of the spirit world and are constantly looking for ways to appease the spirits. In the province of Zambia they would wear charms around their necks made up of teeth of various animals, to keep away evil spirits. Their babies when born would wear a tooth or bead on a spine from an elephant's tail around their tummies for the same reason. At the entrance to their compounds a forked stick dug well into the ground would be seen. Gruesome objects from various parts of animals would be draped over it to guard against the spirit world.

At the secondary boarding school we, as staff, were not without our problems. Involvement in these customs often caused sickness and ill-health among students and their immediate reaction would be to visit a witchdoctor or a local 'medicine man'. They would be given poisonous, evil-smelling liquid to take, concoctions of frogs' legs, chicken livers and roots, which would often put them further into bondage.

When I first went out to Zambia I simply did not believe the stories I heard. I thought it was all in their minds and that they were very gifted at fantasizing! But as time went on I began to realise that this was not so. As a missionary it was my task to make it clear that the Bible teaches that there are two kingdoms – the Kingdom of God and the kingdom of Satan. One is a kingdom of light; the other of darkness. To belong to the Kingdom of God takes away fear and often brings about healing of sicknesses. It brings joy and peace, not fear.

I well remember one particular week had been very stressful. The trouble started in the girls' dormitories when one after another not only felt unwell but had become uncontrollable as they screamed and shook violently on their beds. The local hospital was within walking distance and at first the girls were hastily despatched there for medication. But still it continued and was beginning to spread to the boys' dormitories also. The hospital refused to admit any more students as their behaviour was affecting other patients.

The following Saturday evening I was on duty, which meant that I had to keep an eye on the various activities that were taking place in and around the school compound. Imagine my surprise when the headmaster appeared and stopped all the activities. He sent the boys off to collect wood from the bush surrounding the school and then gave orders to prepare a huge bonfire, large enough for the school to assemble around. He then informed us that a witchdoctor was coming to 'divine the case' and show us who was responsible for the chaos! Here was an educated man with a Bachelor of Science degree still dependant upon the power of witchcraft!

His commands were duly carried out and we assembled round the fire. The witchdoctor then appeared in tattered clothing with a slouch hat pulled well over his face. A titter of amusement went round the school. Two others with him produced a cauldron containing a dark, slimy liquid which they placed on the fire. He then produced from a bag slung over his shoulder chicken livers, pieces of skin and fur and frogs' legs, which he tossed into the liquid. The pot was vigorously stirred with a short, thick stick and the liquid splashed over the crowd. A roar of alarm went up. Immediately the atmosphere changed. No-one was laughing now. As the liquid fell on various students – panic! He then announced that the problem lay in the food which was being poisoned by the cook. He also announced that 80 girls and 40 boys would be affected!

At this the school was in an uproar. Many of the students scrambled for dried grass which they set alight from the fire and with flaming torches ran pell-mell towards the cook's compound. Within minutes his home was razed to the ground. No-one was hurt but the only possessions the poor man had were the clothing he was wearing. What a night! One I shall never forget. And it did not stop there. The screaming and wailing continued all through the night. The next day was Sunday and that morning Gordon Suckling from Sachibondu, and the Catholic priest came to take their respective youth services on the school compound. But very few attended. The witchdoctor had fled and the headmaster too, never to be seen again at that school! The head-boy came to me in despair: "If you Christians who say that the power of God is greater than the power of Satan would prove it at a

Fishing with nets and traps

Typical house on a compound

time like this, we might believe you!" I was devastated. I felt terrible and absolutely helpless. What could **I** do in a situation like this?

Meanwhile help arrived from outside. A medical team came from the hospital to give injections to sedate the worst cases. Mattresses were placed on the floor of spare dormitories and other available spaces. The police arrived to obtain information; the army arrived with fixed bayonets - stretching themselves out on the ground. Laughable really had it not been so serious. Aeroplanes flew overhead as the news had been relayed to other areas on our transmitters. A team of psychiatrists from the Copper Belt landed on our small airstrip but all to no avail. It was like mass hysteria which no-one could stop and it had now spread to the boys' dormitories too.

This continued all through Monday and finally news came from the education authorities that those who lived locally should go home immediately. Vehicles appeared from nowhere and a general exodus followed. A fleet of buses took the remaining students the long journey of 300 miles to various distant towns. Orders were given to stay away for two weeks. We saw the last of the students off on the Tuesday and the bewildered staff took advantage of an extra holiday and disappeared also.

No-one came near the place for two months! Many students asked for transfers to other schools. New students were drafted in and a new headmaster was installed before something like normality returned.

The following weeks gave me ample time to review what had happened. It was a constant worry to me that as Christians we had no answer to this problem of witchcraft. There was no doubt about it, the witchdoctor **did** have power to control with fear and what was more amazing, exactly eighty girls and forty boys had been seriously affected, as we counted the mattresses later.

What was very disconcerting too, I knew that those students would seek advice from other 'medicine men' when they reached home. This was their tradition, so deeply ingrained in them. Even Christian students found it extremely difficult to depend solely on the strength and power that Jesus Christ could give in situations like this. What could be done about it? God answered prayer and the answer came in a remarkable way, as we shall see in the next chapter.

Chapter Nine

Witchcraft

At Sachibondu Bible School, Gordon Suckling often called in elders of the various churches for times of relaxation and further training. On one particular occasion, as they were having a time of worship and praise, one of the leading elders suddenly fell to the floor, foamed at the mouth, stiffened up and writhed like a snake on the ground. As one body, the rest of the men stood up and said to Gordon, "There now **you say** that the power of God is greater than the power of Satan. Here is your chance to prove it!" Gordon was in exactly the same position as I had been in the school and we felt powerless to do anything about it. But Gordon had to act, and act quickly. Remembering what Jesus had done in the Gospels, he took authority on the Word of God and commanded that the demons leave in the name of Jesus. To everyone's amazement, immediately the writhing stopped, the man relaxed and lay still and then sat up, never to be troubled again in that way, as we later discovered.

From that time onwards Gordon made a serious study of how Jesus handled cases of demonic influence and demon possession. He produced notes on his findings, both in English and in Lunda, and gave them to his elders and to any missionaries who were interested. I certainly was because of the situation at the school. Then he trained a team of men in each church to handle such cases in their own districts or areas. People had come from far and wide to Sachibondu to be 'delivered' until it became apparent that the task was too great for the folks at Sachibondu to handle, and that they must remain in their own districts to be healed by their own leaders in their own churches.

Mwinilunga was no exception. God's anointing on some of the women there was so powerful that they too formed teams or joined up with the men. I, myself, teamed up with Solomon at the bookshop and his friend William and often we dealt with cases until late at night. In the end it became just too much, so we settled for Saturday afternoons and used the rooms behind the bookshop, where Hilda Kelly had lived. By this time, the little shop was thriving and these rooms were used for the stock of Bibles, etc. But we cleared one office and held our sessions there.

Similarly at the secondary boarding school, when the students had settled back into a normal routine under new management and any trouble of this nature arose, the headmaster quickly had them removed from the premises. I knew only too well what that meant. Back to the witch doctor. But now we had the answer!

In the course of time, a routine was followed which proved to be successful in most cases. The student was sent to me with a note from the headmaster, "This boy or girl needs help," and was sealed with his stamp. Sometime during the following week I would interview the student. If they were prepared to repent, in the case of Christian students, and not to be involved further in traditional customs which were evil, then deliverance was arranged for them at the bookshop office on a Saturday afternoon. If the student was not a Christian and refused point blank to have anything to do with a total commitment to Jesus Christ and to be filled with His Spirit, then we left well alone. We learned the hard way that setting them free from demonic oppression only made matters worse – as the Scripture says, "His final state became worse than at first" because his life was filled with other deadly spirits to torment him.

There were disadvantages, however, as the shop was in close proximity to the police station and often these sessions were very noisy. It was necessary, therefore, to inform the police of what we were doing. We need not have worried. These men were well aware of the effects of evil spirits and were only too pleased to learn that something was being done.

We were to discover that a number of people, especially men, but not exclusively, had been to witchdoctors for 'hunting rites' which enabled them to be good hunters of wild animals! Consequently, when the sessions started and we took authority over them in the Name of Jesus, they would manifest the nature of a particular animal. Monkey spirits would manifest themselves by causing the person to chatter like a monkey, to scratch under their arms and to lop about the floor. These we bound in the Name of Jesus and commanded to leave the person. We made many mistakes and often went on for long spells with the same person. Eventually we learned that if the demons did not respond immediately, then we did not have the full story or that the 'patient' was still dabbling in witchcraft. Repentance was necessary and counselling prior to deliverance became a very real part of our ministry.

Lion spirits manifest themselves in an amazing way. Hands would become arched like claws, mouths and jaws would protrude and the roar was unmistakably like that of a lion. In no way could these 'signs' be imitated. The person was totally out of control until the spirits were bound and told to leave in the Name of Jesus.

Hippo spirits caused a real problem. The shop was situated close to a river and as soon as the sessions commenced the person would rush for the door and run as fast as he could towards the river – straight in head first! I left Solomon and William to do the rescuing as they chased after him and dragged him out. We solved that problem by having a bucket of water in the room. It certainly worked. The 'patient' would make for the water and empty the contents on himself and on us! Although this was serious business, we could not help laughing at these antics when the person had departed.

But there were other manifestations which had nothing to do with animals. For example, if a man or woman had left their partners and were having a relationship with another person, they were sometimes beleagued with sickness which caused strange behaviour. When they came to us for help, spirits of adultery would manifest themselves in a particular way which enabled us to recognise immediately what the problem was. This saved a tremendous amount of time and again counselling was necessary at this stage.

Eventually, as time went by, the whole district had teams of well-trained men and women capable of handling any demonic situation and deliverance sessions were down to a minimum length of time.

However, one year a bush conference was held at Sachibondu and hundreds of Zambians of all tribes made their way across the country to attend. It took days for them all to travel with their blankets and cooking pots, their Bibles and notebooks. Lorry loads of cheerful people arrived from the outlying areas; others came on bicycles; some on foot; whilst those who could came on public transport. A couple of buses came into Mwinilunga weekly, laden to the hilt. Inside the buses passengers were packed in like sardines, every available space taken. Outside, the roof racks were piled high with suitcases, bicycles, bags of mealie meal, to say nothing of cages of live chickens and the odd goat with its feet tied together! In one way or another the delegates arrived at Sachibondu and settled in their tents or booths that had been specially erected. Booths were made of branches to form a framework which was covered with leaves and sods of turf.

The speaker at the conference was to be Derek Prince, of St. Louis in the U.S.A. He was an eminent Bible teacher and came with his wife Ruth to take the conference. I personally learned much from him but one thing stands out in particular. As the crowds were gathered on the hillside, he asked all the women present who were barren and desired children to stand. I remember recoiling in horror. Surely he was not going to conduct a mass exorcism! Did this man know what he was doing? Did he know anything of the culture of this country? Whether he did or he didn't, he went ahead and bound the spirits of barrenness and commanded them to leave! The balloon went up, as the saying goes, and a mighty cry arose from those women. Many of them fell to the ground slithering and shaking uncontrollably. It was absolute chaos. But then the teams quickly and quietly moved in among the rows and carried the screaming women to other areas away from the conference site to complete their deliverance. Next day the meetings continued as though nothing had happened and we learned later there were those who did conceive and have children who had never given birth before. How we praised God for the training of those men and women who knew exactly what to do. It is a terrible thing in their culture for a Zambian woman not to give birth to a child. It was a common thing and still is for a man to forsake his wife and take another woman if she has not given birth.

But then another vexed question arose. How was it that Christians also had problems? Could it be possible that evil spirits could dwell in a person who was filled with the Spirit of God, the Holy Spirit? Derek Prince believed they could, and he explained it this way:

We are made up of three parts – body, soul and spirit, so the Bible tells us (1 Thessalonians 5:23). Most of us are well aware of our bodies and we do all we can to keep them well-nourished and cared for in so many ways. Our souls are made up of our minds, emotions and our wills. What we allow to enter our minds, i.e. by what we read or see or hear, will affect our emotions and in turn will affect our thinking and the choices we make and the way we behave. Even at an early age, when born, a baby may be perfectly innocent but soon begins to show signs of wanting its own way! The child has a will of its own.

As far as the spirit is concerned, when God first made man in the beginning, his spirit was in tune with God (Genesis 2:15). There was perfect harmony and perfect communication between them. But it was conditional. Man had total control over the garden where he had been placed except to eat off the tree of knowledge of good and evil. If he ate of this fruit he would die. Sadly, Adam, for that was his name, did succumb to the temptation and ate of its fruit. Immediately, his spirit died. Now a great barrier, caused by his disobedience, came between himself and God and he no longer had that perfect communication with God. This became known as sin – wrong-doing.

But God did not separate Himself from man forever. He provided a way back by the sacrificing of an animal – a perfect lamb to atone for his sin. Two things were necessary: a repentant heart and a lamb to be sacrificed by the shedding of its blood. Without the shedding of blood, there was no forgiveness (Hebrews 9:22).

A time came in history, however, when God said He would give His own Son as a final sacrifice. It would no longer be necessary for us to come to God with our sacrifices. The shedding of His Son's blood would be a final sacrifice and we must thank Him for that and allow Jesus to reside in us by His Spirit to lead us and guide our lives. When we do this, the Holy Spirit indwells our spirits and makes us alive to God. Our spirits are then sealed and nothing can break that relationship. Very often, however, we have to live with the consequences of our wrong-doing in the past, but at least we can know God's forgiveness and what peace and joy that brings! *(See illustration overleaf)*

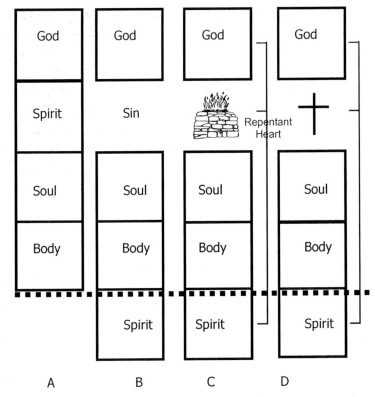

A	B	C	D
In the beginning	Old testament or covenant		New Testament or covenant

A. The first diagram shows how God intended man to be, in perfect harmony with himself

B. The second shows how man became separated from God through disobedience. His spirit died and he was no longer in touch with his creator.

C. But God provided a new way. His relationship with God was restored through repentance and an animal sacrifice that the law required. There was no forgiveness without the shedding of blood

D. Finally God, himself provided a sacrifice by allowing his son Jesus to be the final sacrifice. It is through Jesus that we can now come back to God.

As I look back and remember those amazing years in a government secondary school, I marvel afresh at the power of God in that area. There was so much criticism and opposition at that time but one thing stands out above all else – the Kingdom of God grew as never before. Today men strong in faith, gifted teachers of the Word, and women who were fearless as God performed miracles through them, have passed into the presence of the Lord. But the church has mushroomed and is strong and vibrant today in many areas. I personally was there sixteen years and lived to see this happen.

Village People

Schoolgirls cooking supper at camp

Chapter Ten
Blue Chimneys, Ntambu

At this stage it would be helpful to know the times of the changing seasons. Zambia has three main ones, a very cold and dry spell, when the temperatures can drop very low. I have actually found ice on a bucket of water left outdoors. June, July and August can be very cold, but we never saw rain at this time of the year. This is followed by three very hot months, September, October and November, with temperatures often soaring to over 100°F, especially in Livingstone in the south. Everywhere is dry and barren and bush roads are thick with red, dry sand, making driving very difficult in places. Clouds of dust are thrown into the air by passing vehicles and windows need to be kept firmly closed continually. Even so we found that goods and luggage in the boot would be absolutely covered with the fine red dust unless they had been wrapped carefully with some sort of covering.

The third season is the rainy season which is a blessed relief after the soaring temperatures. We looked forward to the first rains, which fell late November or December, and often continued until March or April.

Tropical storms could be very frightening. Dark clouds would gather ominously above our heads, peal after peal of thunder would rumble in the distance and lightening would zig-zag its way across the skies until the first huge splashes of rain fell. And when it rained ... it certainly rained! It wasn't long before the lawns in our gardens and the paths were submerged. Sometimes the winds would blow fiercely at high speeds, lashing the leaves on the trees and tearing them to shreds. It was not uncommon also to find trees uprooted and sprawled across the bush roads, blocking all forms of transport for days on end. Eventually people would appear from the bush with axes and begin to hack through the trunks until sizeable pieces could be carried on their heads to their huts for their own fires. In my opinion, May was the best month of the year. Everywhere was fresh and green, the rains were over, temperatures were bearable and it was sheer delight to wake up each morning to perfect weather and to know that it would remain like that all day! There was just one snag – the days were getting shorter as the cold season approached. It would be dark around 5:00pm and there was only an hour's difference between the shortest and the longest day in some parts of the country.

No matter what the weather, school holidays were always welcomed at the end of a busy term. Many of the staff headed off to the Copper Belt as soon as their marking of examination papers had been completed. I also was eager to have a break and to get away from the school compound.

Two years after I came to Zambia, a good friend of mine, Helen Whitehead, arrived at a mission station eighty miles away. Helen was a state registered nurse and qualified midwife and a lovely Christian who had a real love for people. At an early age, Helen knew that God wanted her to serve Him abroad. Ntambu was a mission station 80 miles from Mwinilunga with a small hospital with a ward for men, one for women and a children and babies' ward. Ruth Hurrell was in charge of the hospital and Doreen Lane, another missionary, worked with her. Doreen's help was invaluable as she bought the produce grown by the local people to feed the patients. She organised the kitchen, weighed the babies and often helped on the medical side - among the many other tasks that had to be done.

It was eventually arranged that Ruth should meet Helen when she was home on furlough and the result of that meeting was that Helen was to join the team at Ntambu. But not only did they run the hospital, they took Sunday schools in the villages on Sundays, Bible Clubs in schools, camps during school holidays in various districts and daily words of comfort, hope and encouragement were put over the tannoy system into the wards. All these were taken in the local language, Lunda.

The fact that I had long school holidays gave me opportunity to visit my friends there and I really looked forward to spending time with them at the end of each term in their home, which was called 'Blue Chimneys'.

In the dry season, the journey was no problem at all, except the roads were so dusty and everywhere was covered in fine red dust. But travelling in the wet season was another matter entirely. The rains usually fell in November and continued well into March or April. At the beginning the days began with clear, sunny skies. But soon the heat would intensify and by mid-afternoon dark clouds would gather, the heavens would open and the rain pour in torrents. Day after day this pattern followed until the roads became an absolute quagmire of squelching red mud, making driving every bit as dangerous as black ice.

On one occasion, as I was returning from Ntambu, progress had been good as the roads were dry. Suddenly, I ran into a storm in a particularly treacherous part. My little car usually held the road very well, but before I had time to realise what was happening I shot across the road and hit the bank broadside with a resounding thud, only to bounce back again into the middle of the road, half-turning, twisting, slithering and sliding about as I gripped the steering wheel in an endeavour to keep the wheels in the ruts in the centre of the road. But the camber was fairly steep and time and time again I hit the bank and shot back again. I could barely see through the windscreen for the blinding rain. The going was rough as the pot holes were deep and when, at last, the storm had subsided and I came to rest on a firmer piece of ground, I gingerly got out to inspect the damage. To my amazement, I discovered that on the first impact a huge sod of earth had lodged itself in the hinge of the door and consequently had acted as a buffer. Every time I hit the sod of earth, the car immediately bounced off, sending me spinning into the centre of the road. It was truly a miracle. Had there been other traffic on the road, that would have caused further havoc. God had truly been with me on that journey. I was very conscious of His protection as I cried out to Him for help. It is on occasions like this that God proves to be so real.

At the end of the rainy season the entire landscape changes. The trees become fresh and green again as the dust is washed from the leaves. A myriad of tiny flowers in various colours and hues appear between the new, green blades of grass and the bush becomes vibrant with colour. What a wonderful sight! Spring time in Zambia takes on not only varying shades of green but those of red, pink and orange, so similar to the autumn shades in Britain, so spectacular that it takes one's breath away! To the left hand side and to the right, one would find bushland stretching for miles like huge forests of small trees and shrubs with their twisted and gnarled trunks. Shafts of sunlight often played amongst the leaves, casting irregular shadows on the tall grasses beneath.

I couldn't help thinking how the changing seasons of the year are so like the changing seasons of our lives. Times in our youth so full of fun and exuberance, times of growing up when the world around us is changing and we see it with different eyes, times of sickness, sadness and sorrow and times when our physical frame can no longer cope with the hustle and bustle. Yes – varying seasons but every season has its own beauty if we remember that a loving God knows everything, He cares and is in control.

'Blue Chimneys' got its name because the walls were painted a creamy-yellow colour and the chimneys were painted pale blue! It was situated some distance away from the hospital in a large clearing in the bush. From time to time missionaries from other stations would visit here and spend a time of rest and relaxation away from their own work. I thought it was a fascinating place as there always seemed to be a number of animals around. They had an Alsatian dog called Gypsy. He was a watchdog and certainly kept intruders and thieves at bay. Later, when Gypsy died, he was replaced by a Labrador called Shadow. Then there was a cross-eyed cat which had the habit of insisting on sitting on someone's lap only during prayer times and not on any other occasions! Other animals in the house included bush babies which sat inside vases placed on the top shelf of a Welsh dresser, a very clean mongoose which made its

way into the bathroom regularly and sat on the seat of the toilet. It entered the bungalow by means of a ladder placed against Ruth's bedroom window and got through a hole in the mosquito netting. Who taught it to use the toilet? Your guess is as good as mine. Instinct? Perhaps where there was water?

From time to time, people from the surrounding villages brought in animals, especially if they had killed the mother for food and their babies were left. I remember a little grey otter being brought in and as he also needed water, a large zinc bath outside the kitchen door became his swimming pool. How he loved to swim round and round. He lived mainly on fish which people brought until he grew too big for his pool. They named him Smokey. One day he was taken to the Kabompo Gorge and placed in the river there. As he grew bigger he had become quite vicious so he was bundled into the back of their landrover and taken to the river – a lively character now back in his own habitat.

All these animals mentioned so far were free to wander inside and out of the home because they were babies and would have died had they not been cared for. Some were actually fed with a baby's feeding bottle until they could fend for themselves. One day a little blue monkey arrived, Its mother no doubt, being in somebody's cooking pot. It must be remembered that the biggest source of meat came from the wild animals they trapped or stunned with stones from a catapult or even shot. If there was no meat available they suffered, what they called a terrible 'meat hunger'. Some village people kept cows or goats, but they were so scraggy and thin with very little flesh on them. The nearest butcher's shop was in Mwinilunga, where meat from local cows was sold on one morning only each week! So there was no opportunity there to buy.

However, back to the blue monkey. A hutch was made for it near the house and a long chain was attached to the little creature. It was fed on bananas, grown locally, and other fruits and seeds. One day it managed to escape from its chain, having grown considerably bigger. It was Sunday and Ruth, Doreen and Helen and I were all at church down the road. A watchman by the name of Wilson was left to keep his eye on the place. He was elderly but when the monkey got off its chain he grabbed it and held on to it. But with its teeth, the monkey ripped off the flesh from his wrist to his elbow and when we arrived back the poor man was in a terrible state.

Ruth did an expert job in blinding up Wilson's arm and there was plenty of Dettol and iodine around! Suffice it to say, Wilson made a good recovery and the monkey eventually was killed by the village people and I should imagine it also finished up in the pot!

Chapter Eleven

Animal Encounters

Another area in which I considered myself very blessed was to be invited to join an elephant hunt. Living on the edge of a huge area of forest which was part of a National Game Park, elephants would roam, often causing great damage to crops grown by indigenous people living in nearby villages. With their trunks they would uproot trees, tossing them about as though they were mere sticks. They would consume great mouthfuls of foliage and fruit from many trees and roots, often tearing away the bark and devouring that too. They would remain in the forests throughout the rainy season and then move out and spend most of their time in the vicinity of the rivers.

Because of the damage elephants caused to farm land, it was necessary at times to cull them. A licence could be bought for £100 when I lived there and another licence had to be bought to possess a gun.

Darrell Rea took advantage of this and set up camp with his wife and family in the 'bush', often inviting friends to join them. We slept either in our own tents or in grass huts, specially made for us by the local people whom Darrell had trained. The camp would often cover a wide area, consisting of sleeping areas, kitchen, dining room and play areas for the younger ones or a badminton area for the energetic! All this had to be done by 'an advanced party' in preparation for the rest of the campers.

I remember on one occasion being awakened by a snorting round the edge of my tent. A hippo was trying to get in, stumbling over guy ropes, searching for food. My adrenalin glands were certainly working overtime as I lay there in the dark.

Helen, Darrell's wife, an excellent cook, supervised the kitchen and prepared much of the food at home before the camp commenced. Large tins of homemade biscuits, cakes and bread were all baked prior to camp. We were well looked after.

Fishing was a favourite pastime, bream and tiger fish being the most common. If enough fish were caught in one day to feed all of us, then it was fish and chips for our evening meal.

Only the men went on the animal hunts. It often meant trekking for miles into the thickest part of the bush and as the licences to shoot were so expensive, only the largest animals were sought after. Tusks of elephant, rhino and hippo could be sold for high prices. All this has been banned today especially in the killing of black and white rhinos as they are becoming extinct. At one stage there was a very lucrative market for tusks as the rhino ones were used in religious ceremonies amongst certain nationalities, or they were used to make intricate ornaments which were costly because of the ivory. Deceptively, bone was sometimes used and sold as ivory.

Sometimes the men who went on these hunts would be out for days on end, away from the main camp and the women folk. They carried their sleeping bags with them in the dry season and slept under the stars or around a large camp fire. Often animal noises could be heard in the dead of night, the 'laughing' of the hyena, the shrieking of the monkeys or the roar of a lion.

But the shooting of an animal was only the first part of the hunt. It had to be brought back to the vicinity of the main camp and was usually carried upside down with its front and back feet tied together and slung over a pole. Two carriers would then proceed, one behind the other, with the animal suspended between them on the pole, with its ends resting on their shoulders.

Finally came the dissecting of the carcass. The internal organs were removed first and given to those workers who had been on the hunt from the beginning. These entrails were a great delicacy and much appreciated by the recipients. They made excellent gravy to eat with their 'nshima' – a firm porridge made from cassava meal or maize meal, their staple diet. But of course they were to receive much larger portions of meat on the bone, not only to eat in camp but also to take home to their families.

We all enjoyed stews of meat of wild animals even if the flesh was that of a hippo! With the correct length of cooking time, and added herbs and vegetables, an appetising dish could be produced. Some of the antelope types such as impala, puku, kudu, reedbuck and duiker could be very tender and really delicious.

But there is one very sad encounter which involved an elephant which I shall never forget. Some Canadian friends who lived on a mission station had visitors from Canada staying with them. Their station was situated on the edge of a game park. Naturally they wanted to see as much wildlife as possible and a day in the park was planned. It was not long before elephants were seen on the track where they were walking. Anxious to get nearer to take good pictures, they followed them.

Suddenly one of the elephants, a cow, turned to face them, flapping her huge ears and bellowing loudly. They all turned to run back down the track as fast as they could. But the elephant charged after them. As it did so, one of the girls in her early twenties, a visitor, caught her foot in a pothole and fell headlong on the path. One giant foot on her head killed her outright. What a tragedy. Later, it was learned that a baby elephant had been shot by a poacher and in revenge its mother had charged at the first human being in sight.

That evening every mission station in Zambia had heard the sad news by the means of their transmitters and letters of condolence came pouring in. The body was flown back to Canada to be buried there.

Elephants have always been favourite animals of mine and still are, but I remember that event with trepidation whenever I see one. The sheer bulk of the animal, the enormous legs and feet and the powerful trunk cause shivers to run down my spine!

Sadly this same family had great cause to grief on another occasion and related this story whilst staying with me on their way to South Africa to visit their grandparents.

Father and son, with friends, were spending a day white water rafting on a stretch of the River Zambezi which had a series of rapids. The stretches between the rapids were calm and beautiful but on approaching them it was the custom to take the dinghy out of the water and walk along the bank with it to the next level if the rapid was deep and dangerous. Having no experienced guide with them they took risks and consequently were thrown into the water. They swam for the bank but unfortunately father and son found themselves on the opposite sides of the river. On a calm stretch, floating on the water were fishing rods, cameras and other equipment. The son, a fourteen year old boy, dived in to rescue some of the equipment and as he was scrambling up the bank with the last of it, a crocodile came gliding up silently from behind, opened its massive jaws and pulled him into the water. He came up screaming as he struggled but was dragged under, never to be seen again.

As the parents told me this story, my heart went out to them. They would live with the memory of this for the rest of their lives.

Another encounter I had with a dangerous animal was the hippo. It was a common sight to see these creatures in the Zambezi river or in the large pools of its tributary streams or around the islands to be found mid-stream. Frequently they could be seen in the water submerged with just the nostrils, eyes and short round ears above the surface. They are in fact massively built semi-aquatic animals with a large head, barrel-shaped body and short legs with four toes. They have long curved 'tusks' which are actually canine teeth and elongated incisors inside the mouth and are not visible when the mouth is closed.

Hippos have thick hairless skin, greyish-black in colour and when fully grown stand fifty to sixty inches shoulder height. They can weigh up to two tons and a new-born calf can weigh around one hundred and thirteen pounds. Schools of hippos may contain up to forty or more animals and they can be very aggressive, fighting over territory and inflicting severe wounds on each other. They are vegetarian, consuming vast quantities of grass from the surrounding area during the day, then returning in the evening to the water.

It was on such an occasion that I had an encounter with a hippo I shall never forget. Eight of us had been for a game drive and were returning through the bush in a jeep. Suddenly our driver espied a hippo through the trees, making its way to the river. As it had to cross our path, he accelerated in order to get a better view.

Four of us were 'locals' and the other four were Americans on a safari trip. We were all seated in the back of the jeep, four down each side, facing inward. I was the last of our four and was sitting next to the tailgate. The timing was perfect. As the vehicle sped along the path the hippo crossed behind us. Then, without warning, it turned and began to chase after us at terrific speed. As it caught up with the vehicle it made a massive leap for my face, its mouth wide open, showing all its tusk-like teeth. The only thing that saved me was the tailgate and the grace of God. With a resounding thud its teeth clamped on to the metal gate one foot away from my face! With a scream I flung myself across the knees of my companions sitting next to me. Cameras, tripods, binoculars, rucksacks all went flying through the air in the commotion that followed. But the hippo hung on and by this time he was a very angry hippo! He was not going to let go of his prey and hang on he did. But as he could no longer keep up with us, he eventually did let go, leaving a trail of saliva down the tailgate. What a narrow escape! We talked about the event for days and we were so thankful to God for His protective hand upon us.

But there were other members of the animal kingdom that had cause for alarm – cockroaches. One night whilst living in Mwinilunga I woke up with a feeling that all was not well. I was right – all was **not** well. One wall was absolutely covered from top to bottom with cockroaches – huge creatures two inches long. They had entered the room through a ventilator high up on an outside wall. I jumped out of bed, dragging my bedclothes with me, intending to sleep in the next bedroom, only to find that the outside wall there was also covered with these horrible creatures. I ran to the kitchen for a canister of insect spray, appropriately named 'Doom' and sprayed the walls from top to bottom. Then I closed the door and spent the night on the settee in the sitting room. Next morning I gingerly opened the bedroom doors to find the majority lying on their backs, their legs slowly moving in the air as they breathed their last breath. I breathed a sigh of relief at the sight. What an escape! My next task was to sweep up these creatures and dispose of them.

Cockroaches in tropical countries are not necessarily those that live solely in kitchens among food. There are many wild species that live among debris, dead leaves, bark or stones. They love darkness but are often drawn to light. As it was the wet season when this event happened, I guess they took shelter between the cavity walls, through the ventilator.

One other incident is worth a mention, an encounter with army ants. The 'ant' kingdom is very complex. Some are harmless, but others can be very vicious and cause pain. Travelling on a bush road to Ntambu in the wet season, Anne McCrea, a missionary friend from Northern Ireland, and I had been warned to keep to the ruts where other vehicles had travelled in the middle of the road and not to venture to the sides, where the surface was soft and very deceptive. The road was treacherous after heavy rain and in places the ruts were so deep that we were scraping the bottom of the vehicle as we travelled. The camber of the road was steep as the center had been built up to drain off the water.

We had informed our friends at the mission station the time of our departure so that they could estimate roughly the time to expect us. No mobile 'phones in those days! But our progress was slow and without warning we slithered off the main track into the grey mud at the side! With great effort I opened the passenger door and stepped out. I was wearing Wellington boots and immediately I sank into the mud which came well over the top of them. But hidden in the mud were army ants and as the mud filled my Wellingtons so did the ants. Suddenly I gave a piercing shriek. I was being attacked! When disturbed it is the nature of army ants, at a given signal by their leader, to nip. And nip they did! Not only did they invade my Wellingtons, they covered every part of my body. Screaming and yelling, I began to throw off my clothes as quickly as possible. Even to my bra and pants! The pain was so terrible. What a task we had to get rid of them. They had to be hand-picked off my body with leaves until I was clear. Fortunately, no-one else passed us on the track and as we were going to spend a few days with our friends, we had suitcases with us with clean clothes. I was sore for days after that episode and we learned later that a dog had been killed by such an attack of army ants.

But how did we get to our destination? When we did not arrive at the expected time, our friends suspected we had had some mishap and came out to look for us in a Land Rover. They brought Zambian men with them, together with ropes and spades and lamps! By this time it was getting dark. There is very little twilight in the tropics. How glad we were to see them! Soon we were hitched up to their vehicle and pulled out of the mud. But what a sight we were! The back wheels of our car spun round and round, trying to get a grip on firm ground and throwing mud all over us. At length we succeeded and were soon on our way – another forty miles to go! But we eventually made it and after hot baths, good food and medication for the weals on my body, we were none the worse for our adventure.

Animals suspended on a pole

On Safari

Chapter Twelve

Livingstone: A new chapter

Christmas time is a special time for many people, but for those of us who are alone and far from home, we are truly grateful when others open up their homes for meals, companionship and fun. Always on the look-out for such people, Darrell and Helen Rea often invited me to have meals with them or to stay with them during the school holidays.

It was on one of these occasions that I was introduced to Piet and Rosemary Combrink, with their three children: David, Elizabeth and baby Stephen, who were staying with Darrell & Helen. They lived in Livingstone and were spending Christmas with the Reas. Rosemary's mother Violet, who lived in Belfast, Ireland, was a close friend of Helen. Hence the connection. After spending Christmas together, I had a warm invitation from the Combrinks to visit them in Livingstone, little realising at the time what the outcome of that visit would be. Piet and Rosemary lived on their farm 25 miles outside Livingstone and sold beef and chickens to the hotels and shops in the town at that time.

I found Livingstone a sleepy little place, very hot and humid but beautiful with its flamboyant trees down the center of the main road giving ample shade for parked vehicles under their vivid red blossom-ladened branches. The afternoon's heat I found unbearable after the pleasant coolness of the Mwinilunga district. I remember remarking that I was so glad I didn't live there! Famous last words. Most of the shops were closed from lunch time until four pm and then opened late afternoon until evening. They were mostly owned by British people at that time with two or three Indian stores. Goods were plentiful and there were very few things that one couldn't buy.

It was on one of these occasions whilst in town with Rosemary that we noticed a small shop in the process of being built. It was wedged between a bank and a shoe shop on the main road. As progress had come to a halt, we learned that the owner had gone bankrupt. Previously we had remarked how lifeless the town was spiritually. There was an Anglican church, a Presbyterian one, a Pentecostal church, a Catholic one. But one thing was missing, to my way of thinking – a bookshop to buy Bibles and Christian literature.

"Wouldn't it be wonderful to have a Christian bookshop here?" I remarked to Rosemary. That did it! My mind was buzzing with possibilities and for the next few days we could think or talk of nothing else but bookshops!

However, after much prayer and deliberation, we eventually got in touch with the owner and later he offered to let us have the use of the shop and a small office and storeroom at the back. This was for two years, rent-free, if we would complete the building and the painting inside. This we were only too happy to do. But at the end of two years the council refused to give permission to open the shop until electricity had been installed. The owner offered us another year rent-free to install electricity but as there was an acute shortage of cables and wire throughout the country, it was impossible to link us up to the main system. How very frustrating it was for us, but every set-back just made us more dependant on God. We took every problem to Him in prayer until one day the District Executive Secretary surprised us by granting permission to move into the shop without electricity! This meant of course no fans to cool the air and no cups of tea! But this was a major breakthrough. Prayer had certainly been answered. In the meantime, we had not been idle. A carpenter had been busy making bookstands, shelves and counters which were soon in place.

Our small new shop with its central door and a window either side soon arrested the attention of the passers-by. Pot plants, greenery and trailing ivy filled the windows, together with book-jackets to advertise the type of books available. Above the shop a smart new sign was erected 'Christian Book Center'. We were open at last!

At this stage I must introduce John Chikwanda, who at that time was the Distribution Manager for the Bible Society in Lusaka. He lived there with his wife and four children. His job was to distribute Bibles to the various bookshops throughout the country and this involved much travelling and spending time away from home. It was no accident that we met up. I was living in Chingola on the Copper Belt, having taken over the supervision, temporarily, of Emmaus Bible study courses to allow Jim and Rhoda Hess to return to the U.S.A. for medical treatment. While I was there, John called at the house on his way to the north-western province to Sakeji School, where two of his children attended. From this encounter, it became clear that John was looking for a post which involved less travelling and as he was well-acquainted with our source of supply, namely the Bible Society, he was an ideal person to be the manager of the new bookshop in Livingstone. It was to be almost a year before the Chikwanda family arrived. Accommodation had to be found which was very difficult and eventually another house was built on the same plot as mine. Then John took up his new post as manager of the Christian Book Center.

But God had been answering prayer in other directions too. By this time, a former pupil of mine in England came out to work with me in Livingstone. Her name was Joyce Parker. We had attended the same church in Nelson and it was through Joyce that I was introduced to a Christian businessman who owned a card warehouse. Gerry Shorten sold his cards wholesale and stocked every conceivable type imaginable. When we told him about the bookshop, he was willing to send boxes out to us at very generous discounts. They could be shipped out to Dar-es-Salaam and then by rail to Zambia. A container service had been set up by Norman Lane, a Christian businessman, to send goods out to missionaries in Africa. What a blessing that container service became and what a blessing those cards proved to be! We had special stands made to hold them and they brought in many customers from all over the district.

But one thing was essential. We must never lose sight of the aim of the Christian bookshop. It was to make Bibles and Christian literature available to those who were seeking Jesus and to help Christians to grow in their faith. Our number-one bestseller was the Bible itself, of course. We stocked Bibles in twelve different tribal languages, our supplies coming from the Bible Society in Lusaka. We sold all our books at subsidised prices and this we were able to do because of the sale of the cards. Three months later we had sold well over three hundred Bibles in all languages and the demand was growing.

These were exciting days, especially as World Vision International opened a base in Lusaka. This organisation was looking for projects in Third World countries which they could support financially for up to three years. Consequently, when they heard about the bookshop in Livingstone, I was encouraged to apply for a grant, especially as I had now employed three other members of staff to assist with the sales. Carol Kondowe came to work for us as our secretary and Peter Malise was employed as our cashier, totting up items on scraps of paper and rendering change from cash in a drawer until someone bequeathed an old-fashioned cash register with a loud bell when the drawer was opened, until we finally had an electronic one which itemised all purchases and rendered the correct change.

Richwell Mutema was added to the team to keep the shop floor tiles swept and washed and keep the shelves tidied and dusted. At busy times he also worked alongside Peter on the till.

Our work had extended considerably and we were taking books to sell at conferences and retreats which were held locally. The grant was approved and soon we had that little shop stocked to the hilt.

I came to know my staff very well, especially as we prayed together every morning before opening the doors of the shop. We took turns in reading a Bible passage and leading in prayer for the needs of the shop, for customers who were seeking answers to their personal problems – which they often shared with us – and many other situations which cropped up from day to day. These times were invaluable as the staff shared how God had answered their requests and how much more real He had become to them. My aim was to encourage them to become totally dependant upon God, as I had become.

At last the day came when the wiring was completed and there was great rejoicing when we were able to switch on the electricity for the first time! Ceiling fans were set in motion and it was such a relief to feel the cool air circulating throughout the building and have adequate lighting in the darker corners of the shop and in the store rooms.

But we knew that the months and weeks were ticking by and that the owner would need his property at the end of the third year. All this time we had had the premises rent free but now we would have to pay a high rent for this double-fronted shop in the main street or seek premises elsewhere. We had been aware of this from the beginning and had made it a special matter of prayer. God had blessed our little shop in so many ways and we believed it was His will that it should continue. We had also sought the advice of the local council and the only plot they could offer us was on the road behind, which we did not think was suitable at the time.

But, as nothing else was forthcoming, we did accept one which was in a strategic position next to the post office and behind a bank. A spare piece of land lay between the two, but we were not allowed to build on it. It had become a general thoroughfare for folks going to the hospital or council offices.

All this time I had been totally dependent on God financially. I had an allowance of £300 per month from my church in England and every bit of it was spent on books, stationery, posters and cards for the shop. The income raised from the sales was spent on the salaries of the staff and on the rates. A container service which brought many of our cards and books by sea also brought in food commodities which were in short supply in Zambia. These goods were a real blessing to me and often there would be wonderful surprises of luxury goods too. Some of my customers who lived on out-lying farms often brought me gifts of their produce – butter, milk and meat – and whenever I had visitors who needed a night's accommodation I never lacked food for an evening meal and breakfast next morning. "The barrel of meal was never exhausted and the cruse of oil never ran dry." God supplied my need every time. There was always enough.

Apart from paying the staff their salaries, it was my duty to pay for each of them into the National Providence Fund (NPF), which was a pension scheme. But our income made this impossible. Their wages were already under the required standard set by the government but I had supplemented them by supplying each staff member, and their wives and children, with clothing and shoes. They had the first choice of all that came into the shop, which was about every six months. The first garment chosen for each member of the family was free of charge and the rest could be purchased very cheaply. In this way they were made to appreciate what was given, to choose wisely, and to care for their clothing. If they could not afford the garments at the time, they were put aside until the required amount was saved up.

One concern I had, however, was the type of homes in which they were living. Most of them came from absolute hovels and it amazed me how clean and neat they presented themselves at the shop each day. They were from compounds on the outskirts of Livingstone, their whole families packing themselves tightly into two-roomed structures made of concrete blocks. Some of their floors were merely red earth and often the children slept on a piece of cotton 'chitengi', African material, spread out on the floor, no mattress, no pillow, often no blanket and certainly no form of lighting or running water. The women carried the water in huge drums on their heads to their homes from a single tap in the middle of the compound. Some of it was used for cooking and the rest for washing.

These compounds were often miles away and by the time the staff had walked to the bookshop, they were hot and sticky and certainly not in any fit state to serve in the shop. It was essential that they had homes which were much nearer town. So this became our next aim. In the meantime, we added an ablution block with a toilet, washbasin and shower to our premises at the rear of the shop.

Eventually, Carol and Michael Kondowe had a home financed by the Southport Community Church in England. Michael was one of the pastors of the Community Church in Livingstone and Carol worked as our secretary in the Book Centre. A three bedroomed house surrounded by a large garden with orange, lemon, lime and grapefruit trees was made available to us. My church in England offered to buy it and to lease it out to Michael and Carol so long as Michael was pastoring a church. They were to pay the rates themselves. It had three bedrooms, which was essential as they had five children (three boys and two girls). In Zambian culture, boys are always welcomed in the family, as it is through their line that their ancestral family name is continued. As I write this, all restrictions have been removed and they now own the property.

We also obtained another house on a compound near the shop for Richwell and his family, whilst Peter lived with his wife in a couple of rooms specially built for him in the bookshop plot. Peter acted as caretaker and opened up the shop each morning. As Peter's family grew, other rooms were added one by one, until eventually we bought another house for him on the same compound as Richwell.

Outside the shop was a small veranda on which we kept plants in large pots. These gave the place an air of ambience. I taught Peter how to take cuttings and later he developed a small business of his own, selling to the local banks and buildings needing floral displays in town.

Joyce 1960

Chapter Thirteen

Joyce

In the meantime, God had been answering prayer in another direction. A former pupil of mine in England came out to work with me in Livingstone. Her name was Joyce Parker. As her life was so remarkable I shall devote the rest of this chapter to her life story. These are her own words:

> "My life began in the small village of Barrowford, Lancashire, where I attended junior and senior school. I was a deeply sad little girl, very insecure and afraid of anyone in authority. I felt inferior to all the other children for many reasons. The way I coped was to be a bully and with some of the children, it certainly worked, particularly in the junior school. Senior school was much more painful and living a lie on a daily basis was tiring, to say the least! I pretended to come from a home that was similar to the other children's."

I might add, at this stage, that Joyce's 'home' was one of the worst I had ever seen. Her mother was an alcoholic and her father, who earned a decent wage as an overlooker in a cotton mill, was an ardent gambler. They took no responsibility whatsoever for their three children: Brian, Clifford and Joyce. They lived in a tiny terraced house and the children were left to fend for themselves entirely. Brian, the eldest, left home as soon as he had completed school at fourteen. Joyce was neither fed nor clothed and slept on a chair at night. Clifford's bed was a plank of wood.

School days for Joyce were a misery and when not in school, she would roam the streets scrounging food wherever she could and stealing whatever was available. Joyce was a tom-boy and teamed up with a friend called Margaret, who was of similar disposition though from a much better home. They were a wicked pair in the classroom too, always up to some prank or other to disrupt classes and they had no desire to learn whatsoever.

Joyce described the staff with much feeling. She says:

"I remember well each one of the senior school teachers. The headmaster Mr Sharp was a very authoritative man, unapproachable and stern. His wife, also on the staff, was a controlling, bitter-tongued, unfeeling woman who was regarded by most of the pupils as the Head. It was obvious to the pupils that some of the teachers as well as ourselves were terrified of her and I was no exception.

However in all this, although very strict in the classroom, there was one teacher who showed some interest in me as a person. At some point this teacher, Mildred Pratt, invited me to Sunday School. My retort was that as I didn't like school why would I want to go on Sunday too?! But eventually I did go and there I met people who accepted me for who I was and not for what I was wearing."

Joyce began to attend the Central Gospel Mission regularly and after a few months, at the age of thirteen, Joyce heard the words, "God loves you" spoken to the congregation by a preacher one Sunday evening. She said afterwards that she was convinced that he was just talking to her! She said she was "completely bowled over". That night she went home and in a grimy bedroom with wall to wall dirt, no electricity, no bedding, she asked Jesus into her heart. Joyce continued, "God filled that room with a great light and I felt His presence very near. I knew God had heard and answered my prayer!"

From that time onward her life changed dramatically. School teachers noticed that she was attending school every day rather than two or three times each week. The change in her behaviour was so marked that the Headteacher's wife stopped her in the corridor and asked her if she was all right! School became less of a burden to her and although she was never to be an academic student, she did endeavour to make an effort to learn.

At the age of fifteen Joyce left school and went to work in a baker's and confectioner's shop. Here she excelled as all their produce was baked on the premises. The shop was situated in the village of Barrowford, not very far from her home, and was very popular for its sale of bread, biscuits and cakes of all description – to say nothing of fruit loaves and Christmas cakes. Icing too became a speciality and Joyce took it all in her stride and became an expert in these things.

Meanwhile, Joyce's involvement in church life led to a great interest in missionary work abroad. Later she went to a Bible College in London with the aim of going to Brazil with Wycliffe Bible Translators. But it was not to be, much to her disappointment. God had other plans for her life. She had grown into an active young woman, keen on sport, with a beautiful complexion, a unique charm and wit and ready for anything! She had returned to Nelson to live, where she had a flat, but later shared a house with a friend. Eventually she moved to Stamford in Lincolnshire and it was there that we met up again after many years. I was a missionary in Zambia then and was on furlough for a few months. The year was 1983.

Over the years Joyce had suffered with a severe back problem and had had two lots of surgery but to no avail. The procedures were unsuccessful and her condition deteriorated until she became totally disabled. She either lay all day on her bed, which had been brought downstairs, or she sat in her invalid chair which had an extended leg rest. She had been unable to work for sixteen years! But Joyce will tell you they were in many ways the best years of her life, simply because she had to trust God implicitly for all her needs. She had been granted a disabled pension and friends would drop in to chat with her from time to time and to do her shopping and help her in any way they could. But she spent hours alone with her own thoughts and with God. By this time, I was living in Zambia as a missionary and had spent 16 years living in a remote bush area on the Congo border in the North West province. During a few months leave a mutual friend of both of us, Maureen Preston (a nurse) asked one day if I would like to visit Joyce for the day. I was delighted and so we set off. When we met I was really shocked at her physical condition. My heart went out to her. She was in so much pain, her every movement causing such agony.

My thoughts immediately went to Zambia. I had seen so much illness out there - T.B., malnutrition and AIDS – and I had prayed for healing for those people with a group of five women whose faith in God was amazing. What is more, they had seen so many answers to their prayers and seen many people healed.

When I saw Joyce, my immediate reaction was to pray for her and I told her about the prayer group in Livingstone and some of the answers to prayer that we had had. "Would she allow me to pray with her?" I asked. She certainly would be willing and as she replied, an amazing thing happened. God spoke to her in her spirit and said He was going to heal her that day. There was a confidence rising within her that she would no more be an invalid.

As I bent over her and placed my hands on her back and was about to pray for God to remove her pain, I felt God was saying to **me** that this back problem was not a physical one but deep emotional pain caused by her mother's rejection of her as a child. It was a demonic spirit which was causing this and needed to be cast out in the Name of Jesus! I was quite shocked for, although I had both seen and been involved in deliverance of demonic spirits in Zambia, it was a different matter in England. Or was it?

But it was now mid-afternoon and it had already been a traumatic day for Joyce. However, we decided to go ahead and come against this spirit causing emotional pain. I knew no other name for it. All this was totally new to Maureen and as I came against it, Joyce had a very strong reaction and began to squirm and writhe in her chair. Perspiration began to pour down her face. Something was certainly happening. I continued to command, in the Name of Jesus, any demonic forces to leave her. Eventually she began to relax, utterly exhausted but the relief on her face told its own story. Something **had** happened, but I felt in my spirit that she was not totally set free. By this time it was getting late and we had a long drive home as Maureen was on duty the next day. But I felt I couldn't leave Joyce with a task unfinished, so it was decided that Maureen would return home that evening and I would follow, by train, the following day after the task had been completed!

The next day we had another session, beginning at about 10 o'clock in the morning. We took it leisurely as again a great struggle was taking place. But then I remembered something I had found in Zambia, that it had been very helpful if the person concerned 'renounced' the demonic forces herself and commanded them to go in Jesus' Name. This Joyce did and almost immediately release came and the battle was over. All pain was gone but her spine was extremely sore. We prayed again and later that day I left for Southport, where I lived.

I kept in touch with Joyce over the next weeks by 'phone and it was very obvious by her movements that something tremendous had happened. Her account of her visit to the doctor's surgery was very amusing. She had been receiving a pension for her disability but now in all honesty she felt she could not accept it. It was necessary, however, for her doctor to certify that she was no longer disabled. In spite of the fact that Joyce had visited her at the surgery on her own two feet, the doctor was not convinced that she was totally healed and asked her to return in 3 months' time! Then, and only then, did the doctor sign her off and the pension stopped. This was a very brave thing to do as Joyce had no job, nor employment of any kind. Neither had she any qualifications except in confectionary. But Joyce felt that this was not the way forward. She believed God had a greater purpose for her in life. She began to apply to various Bible Colleges and was eventually accepted at one in London. Furthermore, her healing was 100% and to this day, she has not had a back problem again.

Joyce came out to Livingstone for a year and helped me set up the new book shop before returning to England. Later, she moved to Southampton, where she met up and became involved with a Christian psychiatrist, Dawn Brown, who was working with women who had unwittingly been drawn into satanic ritual abuse. These women needed to be released from the power of Satan and to know what it was to be totally set free through a relationship with Jesus, to keep their release. Once a person had become involved in satanic ritual abuse, it was very difficult for them to leave it. Terrible torture was administered to those who made any attempt. Joyce showed me photographs of women whose bodies had been branded with hot irons for not attending meetings in various covens, or attempting to make an escape.

At the time I found it very hard to believe that these things could happen in Britain today, especially as the police were very loathed to get involved and would not believe that these things were happening. But eventually the rituals were exposed and efforts were made to put a stop to them.

Today Dawn and Joyce are colleagues, living in Richmond, New Zealand and are counsellors working with women who are survivors of satanic ritual abuse and those with multiple personality disorders.

This poem was written by one of Joyce's clients, about Joyce:

She taught me that I don't have to live in shadows
Or listen to the vague, accusing whispers.
She taught me not to run away from memories
And the pain which comes from them.
She taught me to look at my hands
And not see filth and obscenity.
She showed me that an outstretched hand
Can mean safety and caring
That there isn't always a threat.
Some people really do care
And that all those moments of darkness
And fear can be faced, with help and kindness.
She taught me that cruelty can be overcome,
Shame lived through, and she taught me that little girls
Deserve love and tenderness, care and understanding.
That the very young are innocent in the crimes committed against them.
She eases my pain and shows me
That not everyone is malevolent, how to be brave,
To stop running away, but most of all
She shows me that despite everything, I really do
Have the right to live.

Chapter Fourteen

The Training Center

It was business as usual in the book shop. We had had a devotional time together. All the staff were present and had dispersed to their various duties. The red tiles on the shop floor had been swept and washed. The books on the shelves had been tidied and re-sorted into their various sections and dusted. The centre stand had been replenished with the latest books on offer and we were all set for another day. It was still early morning and the air was cool and fresh. Soon the customers began to drift in, some on their way to work and knew exactly what they wanted, others had time to browse, whilst the children on their way to school clamoured for biros, pencils and exercise books, while others just needed a sheet of notepaper and an envelope for that special letter.

About mid-morning, two Zambian gentlemen walked in asking if they could see the owner and the manager. As it was not particularly busy, John and I were able to see them immediately. One was a lawyer, the other a businessman. They had come with a specific request. Would we consider taking over a private secondary day school which they had built on a twelve-acre plot? This meant not only the running of the school but the buying of the premises also!

We were to find out later that these two gentlemen were completely out of their depth with that school. They had employed people to teach who had a very limited education and consequently were on very low wages. But when it came to examinations, the results were nil. They came to John and me because we were both well qualified teachers with years of experience behind us.

Our immediate response was to tell them we had no interest in the school. What we required was a plot of land to build a church. Our present premises were too small for our existing congregation. We had in mind a simple structure built on a concrete base with poles round the edge to hold up a metal roof. The sides would be completely open to allow any breeze to blow through on hot sultry days.

The men went away but returned a week later with the same request, hoping we had changed our minds. Again our answer was "Definitely not!". But after a third visit I turned to John and said to him: "John, we are responding negatively to this request but we are not even asking God what He wants us to do. At least we should go and see it. There may be spare land on which to build."

So we called the men back and offered to go and see the place. The whole area was situated on the outskirts of town and only took us seven minutes to walk from our home! When we arrived we were absolutely amazed at what we saw. As we walked through the gateway the buildings were typical of any other Zambian secondary school in that the classroom blocks had an open veranda running the whole length. But each block was surrounded by well-kept lawns, well-clipped hedges and concrete paths. In other open spaces fruit trees grew in abundance – mangoes, papayas (paw paws) and avocados. We learned later that the school had a direct line to the water works. A constant supply of water was evident as everywhere was fresh and green, compared to other gardens in Livingstone.

As we walked around we were certainly impressed by what we saw. There were two rooms obviously intended to be laboratories which would make excellent meeting rooms. The remainder of the classrooms – which had desks and chairs but no blackboards – could be used for Sunday School classes, créche, mid-week activities and youth work. Other areas included two ablution blocks consisting of toilets, showers and washbasins, a tuck shop with a licence to sell to the public as well as the students, and dormitories which would make excellent accommodation for conferences. The possibilities were endless. Land to develop playing fields was also there and large trees giving ample shade were interspersed throughout the area.

Our arrival caused quite a stir amongst the students as we walked down the main driveway. The majority were in school uniforms and looked very smart in their maroon and white pinstriped blouses or shirts and grey skirts or trousers. Rumours abounded that there were going to be changes, possibly in ownership of the school, and the place was buzzing with excitement.

As we looked around I certainly felt in my spirit that we should be looking to God for an answer. Was it His will that we should go ahead and purchase the place or should we let well alone? As in all major decisions, I had learned to wait on God for an answer before I proceeded further. If I heard clearly what God was saying then I had the faith to believe that all would be well and that God would supply every need to bring about His purposes. But there were times when the heavens appeared as brass and my prayers reached no further than the ceiling. Would this turn out to be such an occasion?

This was now May 1991 and I was due to go back to England for a few weeks' break in June. I had planned to return before the end of the year. One thing was certain, I simply did not have the money and before I could embark on such a project, I must consult the Elders of my church in England.

Consequently, I told the owners of the school I would give them the answer as soon as I had seen them. The asking price was £80,000 to be paid in kwacha, the local Zambian currency. At that time £1 = 1 kwacha. They wanted a down-payment of K15,000 by September and the remainder by the end of the year. But I was adamant that should I decide to buy the property, 15,000 would be paid immediately and the remainder would be paid off over the coming year ending December 1992. I knew that it had been on the market for some time and no-one had shown any interest. If God wanted me to have this place, it would still be available on my return – and if the deposit was available I could trust Him for the rest.

When I returned to England I was given a few minutes on Sunday morning to explain the situation to the church. There was to be no pressure to give and it was decided no fund-raising events to raise the money. If the congregation felt it was right and wanted to give towards the project, then an opportunity would be given. One of our leaders held open the pocket of his jacket, saying that if anyone wished to give, by a certain date, would they kindly place a gift or indicate the amount on a piece of paper and place it in his pocket! That very day I had the assurance that the full amount would be given – and it was!

But the story does not end there. The owners of the school did not tell the students that the school was closing down and that they should find places in other schools. Consequently, on the first day of term John Chikwanda and I were astonished to find a large group of irate parents outside the shop with stones and even boulders ready to throw through the shop window!

The students has arrived at the school which was a mile away from the shop only to find not a single teacher or worker were there. They had been given the understanding that John and I were to be the new directors of the school! What a predicament. John in his quiet manner went out to speak to the crowd and to avoid disturbance on the road gathered them on to our property behind closed gates.

The results of this was that we would help the students get places in other schools by giving them testimonials from their exam results! How ludicrous is that? So, for days on end, we saw students off with their references until everyone had found a place in another secondary school. What a fiasco! We had never set eyes on the students before and had to search the school office for examination results and other relevent information and keep the bookshop open at the same time. Can you imagine! An incredible situation.

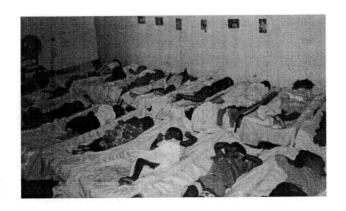

Rest hour at the Rainbow Center, Livingstone

Piet and Rosemary Combrink, Livingstone

Chapter Fifteen

Miraculous Encounters

Livingstone was to become a very special place in my life. Apart from the wonderful way in which God provided for the opening of the Christian Book Center and the Rainbow Center, as it later became known, friendships were forged there which have become very precious.

As indicated previously, I had already met Piet and Rosemary and eventually a visit to their farm became a weekly event when they invited other farmers in the neighbourhood to a Bible Study evening, together with missionaries of other denominations who lived in the area. For me, this was a special treat. As it was on a Thursday evening this involved locking up the Book Center at 5:00pm and heading off to the farm in my double-cab Toyota pick-up, after a quick shower and change of clothes. Rosemary, a trained caterer, was an excellent cook and always had a lovely meal prepared. Another missionary, Eleanor Hunsinger from Alaska, who lived on a mission station twenty-five miles north of the farm, also joined us for supper. Others would come for the Bible Study later and return to their homes the same evening. But I would stay over and sleep there as it was not recommended that I should return to Livingstone alone in the pitch black of night, along an eight mile dirt track and another seventeen miles of dangerous driving on a 'so-called' tarmac road of deep potholes and long stretches of muddy pools in the wet season. But to stay overnight meant an early start for me next morning, at 6:00am, in order to be ready for work at the Book Center at 8:00. But it was well worth the time and effort.

Sometimes we varied our evenings at the farm by listening to Christian testimonies on videos or series of teaching given by anointed ministers such as Rev. David Pawson, Ray McCauley of South Africa and Ed Roebert of Johannesburg, or Charles and Francis Hunter of U.S.A. and Reinhart Bonke of Germany and South Africa. We were so inspired by their ministries and their practical teaching encouraged us to move deeper into the things of the Holy Spirit, especially into the realm of the fruit and gifts of the Spirit, particularly in healing.

Across the road where I lived was a senior boys' boarding school known as Hillcrest. Only the best academic students from across the country were accepted there. Standards were high and the school was noted for its outstanding achievements prior to entrance into university.

Friday afternoons were allocated to clubs and activities and among these was a strong Christian Union where forty boys or so met to pray for the other students, the staff and situations there. Some of the boys had heard about the videos and asked if it were possible for me to show them on Fridays on my premises where the room was set up to show videos. The headmaster, a keen Christian himself, readily gave permission provided they were supervised. So the members of the Christian Union came and, to my amazement, more and more came each week until we were packed to capacity – ninety in all! All this took place in the building where I lived. A foundation slab had been laid for an apartment consisting of sitting room, kitchen, bedroom and bathroom across the width at one end. The remainder was one huge room, intended originally for a church gathering. But as our numbers had grown it had been necessary to move to larger premises. This room was ideal for mid-week groups and activities.

What an opportunity to be able to present to these young fellows, ages between fourteen and seventeen, the way into the Kingdom of God, through the death and resurrection of Jesus and to have a personal relationship with Him every day. They could be motivated and energised by the infilling of the Holy Spirit to travel along the path of life that had already been mapped out for them. They were exciting days and there were those among these young fellows who clearly responded to the call of God on their lives. They were encouraged to attend a local church whenever they could and, on leaving Hillcrest after their final examinations, encouraged to search out a 'live' church in their hometown or wherever their studies led them. I might add that Zambia had many such churches in all denominations.

Through the witness and teaching of many missionaries over past years, both in the towns and in rural areas, the good news of Jesus was widely known in Zambia. Sadly, some churches had become stereotypes, lifeless and legalistic, based on tradition without the fresh touch of the Holy Spirit in their meetings. But other places of worship were on fire for God and were alive and vibrant in their presentation of the Word of God. It was to these churches recommendation was given to the students prior to leaving school, especially those situated on the Copper Belt where the major cities were and where temptations were the greatest.

But there was another group which will long remain in my memory, namely five praying women. This group emerged from a much wider group of Zambian women who met together to pray on Friday afternoons after work at 4:30pm. Our venue was the local museum, made famous for its display of the diary, jacket and hat of David Livingstone, the Scottish explorer who discovered and named the Victoria Falls. The Director of the museum was a Christian and arranged for us to meet in a quiet spot on these premises each week. For one reason or another the group became less and less until there were only five of us meeting regularly. But we were of one mind and spirit and longed to see the outpouring of God's Spirit on the nation of Zambia, our churches and on our families. We really believed that prayer could change situations and people and more than that we wanted to hear from God Himself.

One Friday afternoon as we were waiting on God, Prudence, one of the women, began to receive 'Words of Knowledge'. These are words which God reveals supernaturally to a person, facts which they would have no way of knowing by natural means. Prudence began to tell us that there was to be an attempted coup in the country, to take over State House – the home of the President – with a view to taking over the country. We were stunned, but soon we began to pray and to cry out to God that the plot would be discovered and overthrown. We moved into 'spiritual warfare' and began 'to pull down the strongholds of Satan' to destroy any attempted coup and to bring confusion and disruption on any plans of the perpetrators. In particular, we bound in the Spirit any military activity at all the border posts, as Zambia is a land-locked country with no coast line. Then we waited! Not a whisper of any kind reached our ears. For the next few weeks we listened to the radio and watched the news on TV. We read the newspaper and heard absolutely nothing. Then, we reasoned, if we truly believed that we had prevented a coup from taking place, should we be surprised? Of course not!

Six months later it was reported in a Zimbabwean newspaper that five majors in their army had planned to enter Zambia and advance to Lusaka to take over the country and its government. But the plot had been discovered and the men were arrested and sent to jail to await trial! How we praised God for this timely intervention and for the situation being revealed to us in order that we might pray against it. God truly answered our prayer. We really did believe that this happened.

There were other ways, too, which strengthened our faith. One of those ways was in the realm of healing and we witnessed the bringing to order of a number of physical disabilities. For example, Prudence was totally dependant upon her spectacles to be able to see. The lenses were very thick and the first thing she did on rising from her bed in the morning was to grope for her spectacles! One evening she was sitting at home and had taken them off and placed them on her lap. Forgetting where she had put them, she stood up, only to drop them on the floor. One step forward and crunch! The lenses, being glass, were completely crushed. Great panic followed. It was the only pair Prudence had, as they were very expensive and the nearest optician was three hundred miles away in Lusaka, the capital city. What could be done about the situation? To continue living a normal life without them was impossible. Prudence was with friends at the time and immediately they began to pray that God would restore her sight. Many Zambian

Christians have great faith in God. They simply take Him at His Word. He healed many people when He lived here on earth and He said **we** could perform miracles too if we had the faith to believe that in His Name we could lay hands on the sick and they would recover! So – on the authority of the Name of Jesus- the group commanded her eyesight to be restored. Then they dispersed, believing that the healing had taken place. Prudence retired for the night and when she woke up, the miracle had happened! She was able to see both in the distance and close up without the aid of any spectacles or other devices. Perfect restoration!

Today Prudence lives in London, studying for a PHD, and holds a very responsible position there. Over twenty years have passed since this incident happened in Livingstone. Speaking to her on the 'phone recently, I asked how her eyesight was. "Perfect," she replied. No need of any spectacles whatsoever. Again we give God the glory!

I, too, had a similar experience. Having worn spectacles from the age of eleven, it was a bitter blow to learn that after having had cataracts removed from both eyes later in life, that another skin was forming over the pupils which prevented me from seeing well enough to drive.

It was at an evening meal at the Combrinks' farm that I met two pastors from America who were holding a Healing Campaign in town. One of them, Pastor Pete as he was known, told us how he had been miraculously healed at one of Benny Hinn's meetings in America. He had arrived in a wheelchair, being totally disabled, and had come for prayer. But wheelchairs could not be taken down the aisles to the front of platform because they took up too much room. As he had no other means of getting to the front, he had been given a pair of crutches. The front row was empty and those who were requesting prayer were coming down an aisle, mounting the platform one at a time, where Benny Hinn laid hands on each and prayed for their healing before they returned to their places by crossing the platform and descending the steps at the other side.

In the meantime, Pete had arrived at the platform and was told to sit on a seat in the middle of the front row, which had been left empty. Benny Hinn continued to minister to each person individually, when suddenly he stopped and, facing Pete on the front row, he told him that in three weeks' time God was going to heal him totally. Not only that, God was going to anoint him for a healing ministry himself, where he, Pete, would travel worldwide and minister to thousands of people, many of whom would receive their healing.

So here Pete was, telling us his story at the table as we ate our meal and I was sitting next to him. When he had finished, I told him my story and asked if he would pray for me. "Sure," was his response and so our dinner party turned into a prayer meeting! Everyone in turn prayed that my eyesight would be restored. Nothing happened and I went off to bed.

The next morning the two pastors were up and away long before I rose. The first thing I remembered on waking was the conversation we had had the previous evening. I sprang out of bed and flung back the curtains and lo and behold! I could see the dam and the hills beyond as clearly as can be. I rushed into the kitchen crying, "I can see! I can see!" It was true, my vision had improved immeasurably and everyone rejoiced with me.

Then Rosemary said, "Well, we've had the good news first, now some bad news." She began to tell me that a 'phone call had just come in stating that Doreen Chikwanda had had a stroke during the night and had died on the way to hospital. What a blow! It was so difficult to take in. Only fifty-nine years of age. Doreen was the wife of John, the book shop manager.

I was so grateful that I had visited the family earlier in the week and had had quality time with them. The day was Tuesday and I was due to fly back to England on Friday of the same week. Doreen was buried that Friday morning and her twin brother, Mpundu Mutala, spoke at the funeral. One thing stands out very clearly in my mind. He said that he and Doreen were born at a time when twins were unacceptable. They were looked upon as a curse on the family and if one was a girl, she was the one abandoned or thrown in the river! But their mother was a Christian through the influence of a local missionary. Consequently, she was taught that all life is precious and the little girl's life was spared. So Doreen grew up, knowing her own native language and also speaking English well. She was educated and trained as a nurse and was a fine Christian working among the women in the community and, together with her husband, visiting and encouraging married couples and their families. They themselves had four children, two boys and two girls. Sadly, their first child, a girl, Nisa, had sickle cell anaemia. But beyond all expectations Nisa has survived her mother and is now in her thirties.

I have digressed somewhat from accounts of healing that took place while I was out there but the lives of Doreen and John and their family will long remain in my memory.

This chapter would not be complete without the story of Carol Kondowe's healing. Carol suffered from severe back pain of the upper spine. Around that time we were watching a series of videos, 'How to heal the sick' by Charles and

Frances Hunter of the USA. They taught that sometimes pain in that area could be caused by one arm being longer than the other!! This could be checked out by having the person stand against a wall, shoulders pressed back, heels touching the wall and both arms stretched out in front with palms facing inwards, finger-tips touching. If one was shorter they would take authority and 'in the name of Jesus' would command the shorter arm to grow until the finger-tips were level. This should rectifty the problem and the pain should go.

So, what had we to lose! Carol was very willing and sure enough one arm began to swing forward way past the other and back again. At this the women who were watching began to shout 'Stop, Stop!' as the arm swung forward and backward several times until finally the hands came to rest exactly opposite each other with the finger-tips alligned. And the back pain? Did it go? The next day saw a significant improvment and within a week Carol was completely pain-free. This proved to be a permanent healing as I questioned her a few years later. I might add that pain in the lower part of the spine could be caused by one leg being shorter than the other. After the 'growing out' of the shorter leg 'in the name of Jesus', pain would be eradicated.

Later Carol went to several courses on Child Evangelism in South Africa and is now doing a wonderful work amongst Zambian primary school children holding Bible clubs after school hours. I was privileged to see her recently telling a Bible story to one hundred children, ages three to seven years, holding them spell-bound with a simple visual aid that she had made herself. Quite remarkable and no other adult present.

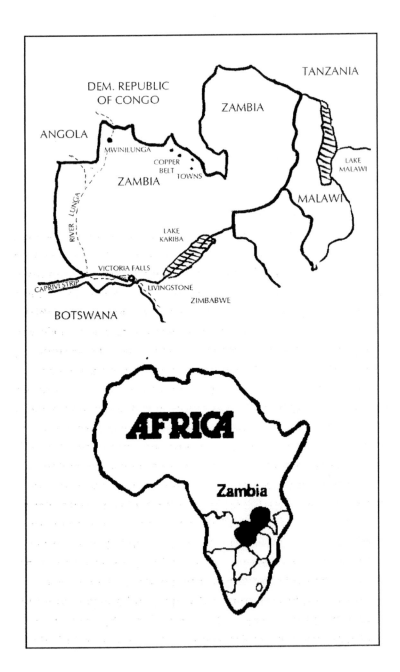

Chapter Sixteen

Bandits

A visit to the Combrinks' farm one Thursday afternoon turned out to be a visit with a difference. I had locked up the shop as usual and was on my way. I had left the main road and was on the farm track. About a couple of miles from the farm, I noticed ahead of me a stationary vehicle. It was Piet's. All the doors were wide open and as I slowed down to pass it, I glanced over to look inside. I was surprised to find no-one in the front seats but in the back were two Zambian women. I noted that on their heads they wore the usual Zambian headdresses of local material and they were staring straight ahead. They made no move to greet me and as I did not know them, I passed by and went on my way. As I drew up to the farmhouse, I was amazed to find all the farm workers congregated outside the back door, which was locked. They were standing in complete silence as I got out of my vehicle. As I approached them, they gathered round me, asking if I had seen the bandits! I told them of the two women in the vehicle but no sign of Piet. Then they told me the incredible story of how Piet had been returning home from town when he was held up by bandits. He had refused to stop and they had fired bullets at him, which had missed but had badly marked his door.

He had escaped through the passenger door and had run off through the bush to get to the farmhouse. Knowing the bush like the back of his hand, he was able to reach there safely, where he emptied the safe and locked all up. Informing the staff of what had happened, he told Rosemary to take another vehicle and make her way to the next farm some miles away. Piet himself took a third vehicle and made his exit along another farm track back to the main road to try and stop me from entering by the usual route and also to inform the police in Livingstone.

But as I had set off a little earlier than usual he had missed me. The farm workers then told me that the two 'women' in the back were the bandits. They had probably heard my vehicle on the road and had jumped into the back seats of Piet's pick-up wearing women's head-dresses.

It appeared that it was Piet they were after as he had reported to the police cattle rustlers in the area, stealing cattle and taking them over the border into Zimbabwe. They were out to get their revenge.

As it turned out, we all escaped without injury and met on the next farm for our Bible study. How we praised God for His protection and goodness to us. In the meantime, the police caught up with the bandits some days later and they were jailed. They had been terrorising various farms in the district, owners and workers alike and everyone was out to get them, and get them they did!

Chapter Seventeen

Essentials For The Task

Looking back over the years, three experiences appear to be of particular significance. The first was when I was baptised in water, completely immersed; the second was when I was baptised in the Spirit and being made aware of the various gifts of the Spirit to do the task of winning people for the Kingdom of God and building them up in their faith; the third was various ways in which I received God's guidance.

Consequently, I have enlarged on each of these as follows:-

Baptism in Water

As a baby my parents brought me to the Salvation Army to dedicate me to the keeping of the Lord Jesus until I was at an age when I could choose for myself. As far as I know, no sprinkling was involved.

Seventeen years later I was attending the Central Gospel Mission in Nelson, and heard Biblical teaching on baptism by being immersed completely in water. This was not a means of membership into the church but was presented as a witness to the fact that a person had repented of his sin and was a believer in the Lord Jesus. Up to this point we had no baptistery in the building but steps were taken to have one built. As I was going off to college shortly after its completion, I was asked if I would like to be baptised as a witness to the fact that I was a new creation in Jesus Christ, the old life had gone and I was now living a new life by the power of the Holy Spirit (II Corinthians 5:17). So, along with two others, I was baptised in water.

During my time in Africa I heard about baptism in water with a different emphasis. It symbolised the death and resurrection of Jesus. As Jesus died and was buried in the tomb, so we too die to the old life of guilt, hypocrisy, jealousy and a whole lot of evil desires as we go down into the water (Romans 6:3-5). In the same way that Jesus rose again from the dead, we too can rise from the water to live a totally new life in Christ which must be nurtured and encouraged to grow. As I listened, baptism in water took on a whole new meaning for me and gave me a real desire to be baptised again. So it was, some forty-odd years later, I was baptised in the sea in a little bay off the coast of South Africa.

I was encouraged to write down on a piece of paper, all the things in my nature that I desired to see changed. I held that piece of paper in my hand as I went under the water and I let it go. It was a wonderful experience and a great cause for celebration. Today baptism in water is encouraged immediately on receiving Jesus Christ as Saviour and Lord.

Repent and be baptised everyone of you in the name of Jesus Christ for the forgiveness of your sins, and you will receive the Holy Spirit.

Acts 2:38

Baptism in the Spirit

Sachibondu River Retreat site will always hold very special memories for me. Not only did it become a place where we as missionaries could escape from a busy routine to rest and relax and hear good teaching of the Bible, but also to meet up with other missionaries on occasions (from other missionary societies), who also needed a well-earned break.

It was on one of these occasions that God began to reveal to us new things, which up to that point had been strictly taboo. "Speaking in tongues" was something that only 'Pentecostals' did. They were a religious denomination who spoke in foreign languages at their meetings. They often did not know what they were saying but when this was the case, there would always be another person there to interpret what was being said. These languages were known languages in many cases but the interpretation would come from a person who could not speak the language himself but was given a divine revelation of the meaning.

Its origin was based on the incident in the New Testament of the Bible, in the book of the Acts of the Apostles. This book tells of the acts or deeds that the disciples did after Jesus had risen from the dead. But they were no longer called 'disciples', which means 'followers'. Now they were called 'messengers', to spread the good news of the Gospel wherever God sent them. Before they commenced this ministry, however, they were told to remain in Jerusalem until the Holy Spirit had come upon them. Fifty days later, at the Feast of Pentecost, a Jewish festival, the apostles together with other 'believers' were praying in an upstairs room when flames of fire fell upon each one of them and they found themselves speaking in unknown languages which they had not learned. They were able to tell the wonderful story of the life of Jesus, His death and resurrection to people in their own language. Furthermore, they received a promise that this gift would be given to their families, their children and to future generations – in fact to all who truly desired the gift and would call on the name of Jesus for the forgiveness of their sins.

Here we were at Sachibondu, being reminded of these facts and being challenged to receive this gift and to be equipped, energised and motivated by the Holy Spirit to not only tell others about Jesus but to be able to praise and worship Him in a new language and to move in other gifts of the Holy Spirit. We were encouraged to 'lay hands' on these who had illnesses in order that they might recover.

It was some time before I received the gift of tongues. I dearly wanted to speak in another language and people prayed with me but to no avail. It was not until I returned to Mwinilunga and was alone in my bedroom one day that I suddenly had the urge to 'open my mouth and try to speak', when the language just flowed. Since then I have had no problem. Sometimes I use it in sheer adoration, worship and praise to Jesus for who He is and what He has done. At other times it is useful to break the power of satan in spiritual warfare or in the healing of various diseases. I must add that when I use the gift for this purpose, the language is different and I can only assume that it is another tongue. Whatever it is, it is very uplifting and I truly believe it bring glory to the name of Jesus.

When called upon to cast out demons, I have discovered that nothing disturbs the demons more than when I speak in tongues. They will often respond to the 'tongue' by pleading not to speak in that language or to mention the blood of Jesus. But it is advisable not to hold conversations with demons but to get on with the business quickly of ousting them in the name of Jesus. Powerful stuff and speaking in tongues is a powerful weapon.

Gifts Of The Spirit (I Corinthians 12:7-11)

The nine gifts of the Spirit fall generally into three categories.

First, there are the revelation gifts:
1. The message of wisdom
2. The message of knowledge
3. Distinguishing between spirits

Second, there are the power gifts:
1. The gift of faith
2. The gifts of healing
3. The working of miraculous powers

Third, there are the inspiration gifts:
1. The gift of prophecy
2. Speaking in different kinds of tongues
3. The interpretation of tongues

All these gifts are given to those in the Kingdom of God for us to use as the Spirit directs us. Much could be said on each one but suffice it to say that should we should eagerly desire them in order to build up each other in our walk with God.

Guidance

It is not always easy to know God's guidance in a situation, but I have learned over the years that the main thing is to surrender one's will to God. This is priority. Some of our choices are not between right and wrong. Both ways may appear to be right and it is all too easy to have our own preconceived ideas of what we want and then ask God to bless them, as the right way. But should our ideas be at variance with Biblical teaching, then the answer is simply, "No". I had a little 'formula' which I used when faced with big decision-making:

1. To surrender my own will to the will of God before any decision is made and to ask Him to close all doors to avenues which are not right for me and to open up the way that is right for me.

This is not a crutch on which to lean. I believe this shows true faith in God. He sees the situation from beginning to end and I trust Him to bring about His purposes for my life in His own way and in His own time.

"For my thoughts are not your thoughts, neither are your ways my ways," declares the Lord. "As the heavens are higher than the earth, so are my ways higher than your ways and my thoughts than your thoughts."

Isaiah 55 verses 8 & 9.

2. Most major decisions are made through an inner conviction to do a certain thing. Very often that conviction comes from God and as we pray that God will confirm, the conviction grows stronger.

3. A third way of confirmation is through God's Word, the Bible. If we are truly seeking God, He will confirm through Scripture - which may come in various ways. A verse or passage may crop up in our regular reading of God's Word. On the other hand a verse on a calendar or on a plaque on the wall of someone's house may be another way which God uses to alert our attention through His Word. An article in a Christian magazine may be a possibility or it might simply be a direct appeal for a cause or a need which stirs us. In whatever way God desires to get our attention, He will do so.

4. But often it is circumstances finally which govern our decisions. As I look back, for me, God's guidance was certainly along these lines. I had been made aware of the need in Africa through Len Moules, a speaker at the International Revival Convention held annually in Southport. More specifically, the need to replace Hilda Kelly teaching in a government school in a remote bush area in Zambia was made known to me. This later was confirmed as I was accepted by the Zambian government as a missionary and granted a house on the school compound. But above all I had continued assurance and peace of mind that I was on the right track. It all fitted into place that my guidance was right and it was!

1. **C**onviction to do a certain thing
2. **C**onfirmation from God's Word
3. **C**ircumstances often follow
4. **C**rowned with peace of mind

Honour from the Queen

A visit to Buckingham Palace

Chapter Eighteen

Honours from The Queen

There is one other thing that I must share with you. At the beginning of the year 1994 I began to feel the time had come for me to leave the work in Zambia and return to England. After twenty seven years spent there ,sixteen years in the remote area of Mwinilunga and eleven years in Livingstone, the call to return was just as clear as the call to go out there in the first place.

My church in Southport had faithfully supported me financially for the past nine years and as I had been very unwell over the last four years it was decided that I should have longer spells in England in order to acclimatise to the unpredictable weather! So this is what I did until April 1st 1994 Good Friday which turned out to be the coldest Easter for a century! But I was so blessed to be able to return to the warm spacious flat that I had known for the past six years. I went down with influenza almost immediately. Then a month later I was rushed into hospital and had two major operations within a week. One was a suspected bowel obstruction which turned out to be a growth on an ovary which had turned gangrenous. These were removed and six days later another operation on the bowel was necessary I was in hospital five weeks plus two more in a rest home and a further week with a good friend Barbara Pratt (no relation!) before returning home. It took me a whole year to recover.

Then came a big surprise. A letter arrived from the office of the Secretary of State for Foreign and Commonwealth Affairs asking if my name could be submitted to Her Majesty the Queen for appointment as a Member of the Most Excellent Order of the British Empire ...an MBE!! This was in May 1999. Who could refuse such an honour?

Later I learned that my name had been submitted by John and Maureen Preston of Garstang, Lancashire, after a visit to the area. My grateful thanks to both of them and to Dorothy Taylor and John Sutton-Smith who were also involved in bringing this about.

So it was that on December 7th of that year I received a medal from Queen Elizabeth at Buckingham Palace for work achieved for the people of Zambia. Three friends were allowed to attend the ceremony with me. What a difficult choice that was. My brother Stanley was first choice and Hilary Hobson, who was sharing my home at that time and Helen Burton, a close friend, joined me on that very special occasion.

I am often asked if I miss life in Zambia and I can honestly say that I do in many ways – the friendliness of the people and their eagerness to learn, the lifestyle, the daily routine and most certainly the weather. But I was also aware that God was calling me back, not to retire but to a change of direction in another sphere and to be available to Him wherever He might lead. And I can honestly say there is no greater place than being in the center of God's will!

Since then I have returned to Zambia both to the Mwinilunga district and to Livingstone from time-to-time and it has been a real joy to see spiritual maturity in many of my Zambian friends. But sadly some of my closest friends among my colleagues and of the farming community are no longer with us. Eunie Fisher died in 2002 after a serious illness, Gordon and Peggy Suckling are no longer there; Darrell Rea died shortly after a 'plane accident in 2005 and Helen died four months later. For me it was an era that had come to an end in the Mwinilunga district. Things would never be the same again.

Meanwhile, in Livingstone the Training Center had been taken over by Ewart and Christine Crowther from Loughborough and renamed Rainbow Africa. Over the next few years the twelve-acre site developed in an amazing way. A trust has now been formed, Rainbow Trust Africa, its aim being to improve the lives of the people by providing health care, education from pre-school to secondary school, AIDS awareness programmes and more informal training in disease prevention and basic life skills.

Today, it boasts of a medical center with a low-cost, high quality clinic and a mobile clinic taking health care to rural communities where access to health care is minimal. It also works in conjunction with Vision Aid to provide free eye care and spectacles annually. In recent years a maternity unit has been opened.

Sadly, in November 2005, Christine died of cancer at the age of 61, which was a sad loss to Ewart and his family and indeed to us all. But Ewart has continued to minister to the people of Zambia in many ways, opening up other centres between Livingstone and Lusaka, bringing help, employment, homes and care in a very needy land. A school library is now in construction on the Rainbow Center in memory of Christine and in recognition of her work over the years.

In April 2008 Ewart married Hilary Hobson who was heading up orphan work with Global Samaritans USA, in Zambia. They are based in Loughborough, Leicester, UK, and return frequently to Rainbow Africa to continue the work there. There are now eighty workers on site.